Joy Writing

Also by Kenn Amdahl:

Algebra Unplugged, (with Jim Loats, Ph.D)

Calculus for Cats (with Jim Loats, Ph.D)

There Are No Electrons: Electronics for Earthlings

The Land of Debris and the Home of Alfredo

Joy Writing

Kenn Amdahl

Clearwater Publishing Company

Clearwater Publishing Company, Inc
PO Box 778
Broomfield, CO 80038

www.clearwaterpublishing.com

Joy Writing
Copyright Kenn Amdahl 2005
All rights reserved
ISBN 0-9627815-2-5

Printed in the United States of America

Contents

Improving

Acknowledgements

Many thanks to my family members who read each version in turn and offered kind and perceptive suggestions: Cheryl, Paul, Scott and Joey Amdahl. They are the reason I write or, for that matter, do anything at all. Special thanks to Joe Reid for editing. Thanks to Jim Loats for the brilliant idea of including examples.

Thanks to all my writer friends for suggestions, support, encouragement, and listening to me whine, especially Liz Hill, Joel Reiff, Ruthie Rosauer, Lynn Skinner, Irv Sternberg, Alan Stark and Alan Bernhard; plus the members of the Colorado Independent Publishers Association, Rocky Mountain Fiction Writers, Colorado Authors League, and Publishers Association of the West. In fact, thanks to the entire Colorado book community, which you can visit via links at www.coloradobook.org.

Muchas gracias to all the writers who allowed me to use their words. It was a cheap trick, I admit it: making this book seem like it had a lot of fine writing in it by borrowing from my betters. I tried to use snippets that would encourage readers to seek out their works without infringing on rights, and have tried to get permission from each writer represented. If I missed someone, and you discover your words herein, and it bugs you, please don't sue. Just let me know and I'll remove them from subsequent printings. My hope is that new readers will discover your work because of the sample herein, and their lives will be graced like mine has been as a result.

I appreciate writing books and their authors, especially Willam Zinsser's *On Writing Well*, Annie Dillard's *The Writing Life*, and Ray Bradbury's *Zen and the Art of Writing*. Three books from different universes. I also thank Dan Poynter for *The Self Publishing Manual*, without which I'd still be sending out queries and collecting rejections.

I know I've got many friends out there I've never met, folks I've exchanged e-mails with, people who have read my books and felt a momentary connection. There is no way to express the gratitude I feel to people who have read my words. To you and to all the book buyers in stores and libraries (most notably Marcella Smith of Barnes and Noble) who have kept me safe from a Real Job, best of luck to you. May all your ventures prosper, all your books be important, and may your critics be widely recognized as the tasteless fools they are.

Kenn Amdahl

Introduction

Sooner or later, many writers feel the urge to write a book about writing. For some, this may be a celebration of their expansive ego. But most, I'd bet, share my situation: so many friends, relatives, and strangers ask me to comment on their work I find myself repeating the same ideas over and over again. Wouldn't it be more efficient to write down my opinions and pet concepts? Wouldn't it be kinder to hand them a book than to surprise them with strong opinions they could not predict? Wouldn't it be better to say, here, this is what I think about writing. Take it or leave it.

That's what this is and nothing more. It's not a comprehensive textbook; it is not a stone tablet sent down from some elite literary temple. Some smart people might disagree with parts of it. Before an indignant reader posts a review on Amazon.com saying, "What gives this clown Amdahl the right to represent himself as an expert?" let me say this: I don't and I ain't. I'm just a guy lucky enough to have the best job in the world, writing. This book explains how I do it.

Many people have found these ideas useful. I hope you do too.

Before You Write

Why Write?

There's a party in my basement populated by the most intelligent, interesting, and creative people who have ever lived. As I sit outside, alone on my chilly patio, the sounds of laughter and eager conversation tug at me. I nearly put down my writing implements and join my friends, but for a moment I resist. The party won't calm down before my fingers tire and my brain is empty. Anyway, I can picture what I'll see when I go down there:

A silver-haired gentleman in a white linen suit reclines in the most comfortable chair regaling those around him with stories of his childhood in India. A jolly red-faced man, whose shirt won't stay tucked in, tells a joke then laughs loudly at his own punch line. A bright-eyed woman, who believes in all things supernatural, tosses her hair and convinces the rest of us to believe what she believes, at least for a while. A young man with a deep solemn voice speaks simple phrases that don't quite make sense, yet sound important. A pretty girl flirts outrageously.

Many of my guests are dead, but it doesn't matter. They live in books that line my walls – the books they wrote. When I open the pages, I'm by their side, listening raptly, watching them gesture and smile, living their lives with them once again. It's an irresistible party with only one drawback: they can't hear me. And so I sit on my patio and write my responses to them, clumsy and hesitant. I want to be part of their community. Of course there is honor in being an attentive listener or an avid reader but sometimes we need to speak back. So we write.

A carnival kind of magic resides within a well-written book. It intoxicates, confuses, delights, and hypnotizes the susceptible until they have no choice but to join the traveling show. Utterly drunk, they long to pull the curtain back, learn the incantations, and climb on stage. Given the right hat, they know they could extract a rabbit from it.

Most literary magicians who work the back roads in bright caravans never become Merlin or Houdini. Or Shakespeare, or Steinbeck, or anyone else you've ever heard of. Few writers aspire to greatness, fewer expect to become rich. Those are excuses we give friends to justify our addiction. We write because it's so much fun, because we are compelled to, because it's in our nature. When asked why he wrote such gruesome stuff, Stephen King replied, "What makes you think I have any choice?" He did not choose his writing life. It chose him. Most people write, not for money, fame, or extra credit on the final exam. It's more basic: once we learn to ride words around the block without skinning our knees, it's a blast.

No one can remodel you into a writer nor can anyone prevent you from committing random acts of literature. If you've got this book in your hands, you're probably already a wild-eyed addict, furtively sneaking words into sentences when no one's looking, rationalizing your actions, telling yourself you can stop whenever you want.

The first step is admitting you have a problem. The second step is constructing excuses, rationalizations, and plans so you may continue writing without the guilt.

The brilliant solution is to try to improve. In one master stroke it satisfies friends and relatives and makes you feel better. If you're trying to improve, snobs and relatives will cut you some slack, hoping you become so rich and famous you'll buy them a car. If you improve, you might win a big literary prize and invite them to elegant parties. You might get published and recommend their book to your agent. With this plan, it doesn't matter how well you write today. Your art is a work in progress, a living thing under-going metamorphosis, too fragile for the harsh light of criticism. Yes, writing is just a whole lot more respectable if you're trying to improve. But how?

It's not difficult to learn tricks of misdirection to work into your act; just remove yourself from the audience and watch from backstage. Notice when you find yourself most engrossed by a writer you admire, then pull yourself away and ask, "What did she do that worked so well?" Don't ask as a reader, a member of the

16

audience, but as an apprentice. That's how people improve their writing skills: by playing detective. Every writer leaves clues, fingerprints, secret codes, and treasure maps in their writing. All you have to do is notice them.

Words are a writer's only tool yet many writers ignore them. They worry about plot, pacing, and characterization. They learn about submitting their work, getting an agent, formatting a manuscript. Then, exhausted, they hurl the words themselves onto the page like garbage. The plot was great, the ideas revolutionary, but the book was unreadable. So we're going to discuss words. If a book works for you, read it again, this time like a writer, and figure out what the author did with the words. How long were the sentences? How active were the verbs? The same tactic works on elements of plot, pacing, tension, and character development. We'll discuss those a bit as well, just to illustrate how to do your own detective work.

My goal is not to strip you of your originality by insisting on one correct way to write. The goal is to free you from the automatic writing that makes you sound like everyone else.

This book is a summary of my own observations about the magicians I admire. Its single idea is this: observe masters *you* admire to see how they use language, then steal their tricks. Why learn from anyone but your own favorite author?

Writing and reading are related activities, but not identical activities. Both send us on vacations from our everyday lives, for example, but no one complains about reader's block.

A great vacation provides contrast to our daily lives. A lifeguard might yearn to go skiing; a ski instructor may fantasize about the beach. Writing's better. When we write, not only do we choose the setting, we also choose to become whomever we want and vicariously experience things absent from our daily lives. Readers take books to the beach to read. Writers take paper (or laptop computers) to the beach to write. Both readers and writers want to live an alternate life, to travel the road not taken, but writers want to be in the driver's seat, not the passenger seat.

Both reading and writing engage our emotions, but in different ways. A well-written article or novel activates our emotions, as if the author is consciously directing them. Most of the time they aren't. When a writer tries to manipulate our emotions we usually sense it and get irritated.

Rather, writers use the act of stringing words together to process their own emotions, much as they might use a therapist. When writers feel sadness, or loneliness, or joy, they release these emotions with words, often writing things that have no apparent relationship to what they feel. When they're done, remarkably, the sadness or loneliness has softened, the joy has intensified. It only seems to work in a positive direction. Unless you are Sylvia Plath or Virginia Woolf, you never feel worse. If you find yourself feeling worse, get a new habit. You're allergic to this one.

This may be the best-kept secret of the writing community. We don't write to make you feel good, we write to make ourselves feel good. If you discover this also works for you, you won't care how much money you make with your words, or how much fame you collect. It's the cheapest drug in the world and one of the most effective. If you're susceptible, it will hook you. As Terry Brooks, author of the Shannara books, says in *Lessons From a Writing Life: Sometimes the Magic Works:*

If I don't write I become restless and ill-tempered. I become dissatisfied. My reaction to not writing is both physical and emotional. I am incomplete without my work. I am so closely bound to it, so much identified by it, that without it I think I would crumble into dust and drift away.

Does that sound like a guy who writes for the money or good grades or fame? Does he write to make you, the reader, happy? No. He's just like you and me, a guy who has discovered a way to stay out of the loony bin by writing, and it wouldn't matter much if no one ever bought his books. He'd still write.

Skillful authors divert the power of their emotions onto the page where it can't harm them. When they feel pain they write pain and the reader feels it as well. Learning to craft vivid sentences takes practice but this tapping into your own deep well isn't enforced drudgery, like learning to play golf. It's not some trick of intense concentration, it's a form of practiced relaxation, much more like meditation.

You don't make yourself write, you let yourself write.

Rituals

Okay, so I call them "rituals," which conjures an image of mystery and magic. You might call them "habits." I like to think of myself as a witch doctor or Mayan priest rather than a mere creature of habit. Defining one's idiosyncrasies creatively is a valuable benefit of declaring oneself a writer.

When I joined a health club, I decided to harness my admirable tendency to repeat behavior patterns. I didn't give myself the goal of working out every day, which sounded intimidating. I didn't set improvement goals either, like "double the weight I lift in one year." That kind of goal sets up a fellow for failure and stress. You could work out six days every week, improve your health dramatically, and win the Boston Marathon but still think of yourself as a failure if you set goals too high. No, I didn't want to risk winning a marathon and still thinking of myself as a failure.

So I set my goal as "visiting the health club every day for a month." If I walked into the club and took a shower, I checked the day off on my calendar, whether I exercised or not. Perhaps because the club had a steam room and hot tub, I met my goal. If I actually sat on an exercise bike or hoisted some weights, I gave myself a big pat on the back for exceeding my expectations. I wasn't trying to get in shape, at least not directly. I was trying to make exercise a habit. By the end of the month the pattern was so ingrained it was harder to skip the trip to the health club than to go.

I employed the same self-trickery when I decided to write my first book. First I listed all my goals: win a Pulitzer, become rich and famous, etc. As I thought about it, I realized I actually had many smaller, more reasonable goals. The Pulitzer would be nice, but not too likely. I'd be happy if I just wrote a good book. Of course, I had no reason to think I could write a good book, but deep down, that wasn't even my primary goal. When I got down to my most basic motive, I realized that I wanted to remove myself from the category of "people who would like to write a book" and place myself in the category of "people who have actually written a book." The other goals all flowed from that. I couldn't write a "good" book if I hadn't written any book. I couldn't make money on a book if I didn't publish one and I couldn't publish one if I'd never written one. After careful consideration I decided that the key to all the other goals was simply writing a book, any book. It didn't have to be good, or publishable; I could fix it later. Even if I couldn't, at least I could call myself a writer.

This felt liberating. I wasn't at all sure I could write a good book, but I knew I could write a bad one. All I had to do was fill two or three hundred pages with words. Writing a bad book doesn't require genius, just typing skills – plus the same kind of determination that forced me to go sit in that hot tub.

Like most people, my days were already filled with making money, keeping my car running, and checking my e-mail. I couldn't just drop everything and write all day. But I had time to write three pages every day, especially if those pages could be filled with terrible writing. In three months I'd have a book. Then I'd turn to the other goals.

I set aside a small block of time every day and chose a spot where I wouldn't be disturbed. I selected a special pen I would use only for this project. I probably wore a special writing shirt and sipped coffee from a designated writing cup. In my assigned place, at my assigned time, wearing my writing vestments and drinking from my porcelain grail, I had no choice. I lit incense and performed the holy ritual of writing badly.

As the days passed, I began looking forward to this time. All the goals that were based on what other people thought of the book faded away. Even if no one ever read it, this was more fun than watching television, more fun than anything I could think of. Why hadn't anyone ever told me about this?

Many people plan out their books in detail before they ever write a word. They make the excellent argument that this saves them from writing pages that will be discarded once the book takes shape. Others plunge in, because it's more fun to write without a road map, and they figure they'll have to revise it all later anyway. I find myself in the middle. I usually have a plan, but it's loose; more a set of suggestions than commandments. Most important for me is to put words on the page. Three pages a day seems easy, like I'm not really doing my job. Five pages feels about right. By the time I've written five pages I'm ready to go mow the lawn. I've written as many as twenty pages in a day, but not often. I write with a pen, and after that many pages my hand is simply too tired for it to be fun. Some extremely prolific authors write a single page a day, but they never take a day off. Think about it: that's 365 pages every single year of their adult life, which could be more than sixty large books. For my first book, I wrote between three and ten pages every day.

Three months later, I had a new addiction and the book was done. I knew it wasn't very good, there was much to be fixed, but I treated my family to a little celebration. I was no longer a guy who wanted to write a book. I was a guy who had written a book.

Now I'm a guy who's been making his living writing for many years, but time has not dimmed the glow surrounding that first accomplishment. No money changed hands, no prizes arrived, yet it felt like I'd just kicked the winning field goal in the Super Bowl. Wow, I thought. I wrote a book.

I want you to have that feeling too.

Beginning to Write
Creativity and First Drafts

Write Badly

Writing is easy, but writing well feels impossible. The goal of "writing well" scares us into silence. We can't write perfectly – the goal recedes before us all – yet everyone expects to.

You don't make this mistake in other arenas. You don't expect to win the first time you bowl or play basketball or chess. No one expects to be a concert pianist the first time they touch a piano. They take a few lessons, hit some clunkers, and practice. Those who love the time spent banging on the keys practice more and try to improve. Some become musicians; a few make money at it. For the rest, the pleasure is worth the scales. Few golfers support themselves by playing; most spend millions of hours whacking at balls for free. They do it because in their perverted worldview it's fun, just as writing is fun for sane people.

The problem is that you already write, you've been doing it since first grade. It seems a tiny leap to churn out a weekly column or type up a quick mystery novel. How hard can it be? Read a couple of books, make an outline. You write about as well as anyone already plus you're a fast typist, so you have an advantage right there.

But it's not a tiny leap for anyone. Not even Tiger Woods was "Tiger Woods" when he began. Steinbeck wrote three unimpressive novels before he found his stride. Many people write one thing, realize it's bad, and give up. Others write something they love, someone tells them it's bad, and also give up. Either way, the world is saved from one more writer.

I'm here to tell you it's just fine to write badly. Embrace your clumsiness, laugh at your mistakes. Your first draft is *supposed* to be bad. That's the second Big Secret writers would just as soon keep private. Nearly all of us churn out terrible first drafts we would not show to a corn slug.

Most writers revise relentlessly. We write a sentence, painfully aware that it falls short, then press onward despite the stench from the words we've already disgorged. Later we locate chunks to discard, we upgrade vague words with more precise ones, we trim fat.

Resist the temptation to impose standards on your writing. Instead, let yourself write badly knowing you can fix it all later. Premature standards kill all the fun. The more words you write, the more graceful you will become. You'll remain awkward only if you fail to write.

Writing and revising use parts of our brains normally locked in endless warfare: the creative genius and the evil dictator. Writers have recognized both characters for centuries, we just give them different names.

The ancient Greeks called the creative genius "the muse" and pictured a ghostly sprite who visited them with inspiration. They considered the muse a god. Some people talk about their "inner child." For writers, "inner child" is another name for the muse. Like any child or ghostly sprite, he's messy, undisciplined, and fickle. I think of my inner muse/creative genius as Bart Simpson, the wisecracking brat from the popular cartoon show *The Simpsons*. That may explain a lot about my writing

The evil dictator also has many names. He's your inner parent, a stern teacher, the rational adult aspect of yourself. Most people think of him as the editor within them. My own adult-inner-editor is no match for Bart Simpson. I think of him as Colonel Klink, the comical Nazi prison warden on the old TV show *Hogan's Heroes*. He was strict and precise but easily fooled. Yours may be much more powerful.

Writers need both characters.

The playful child inside you, who likes to finger-paint and throw mud at walls, creates the first draft of every essay, letter, book, and poem. He's the only guy on your team who can write original sentences. He's a loose cannon, but you need him. Unfortunately, this inner Bart Simpson, despite being unruly, wild, unpredictable, and rebellious, is remarkably vulnerable and easily discouraged by criticism and rules.

Editing and revising is done by the grown-up in you who reads books, obeys rules, and sends cold food back to the chef. He (or she) scolds rambunctious children, argues with parents or a spouse, and complains when over-charged. Colonel Klink understands rules, proper procedures, and following orders. He (or she) doesn't fool around.

That part of you can't write. It can correct spelling and punctuation and criticize when you color outside the lines. It recognizes flaws, but can't fill a blank page to save its soul.

Lock Colonel Klink into a closet while you write the first draft. Bart won't sling any mud if he's being watched. Don't let your internal editor criticize your finger-painting or let it order you around. It shouts words like "should," "can't," and "must." All the "rule" words. You *should* write like this, you *can't* say that, you *must* do this. Once those words are uttered, the blank page wins. The child withers and slinks away, obedient but silent.

A strong internal Klink makes first drafts difficult. He points out flaws before you even finish writing the sentence. Some professions require a strong internal Klink, and people in those professions have a special challenge.

Attorneys practice precise writing so much they often have trouble writing anything but legal briefs. Teachers become so accustomed to correcting their students they can't refrain from correcting themselves. As professional editors read, they constantly look for flaws to repair and notice the most harmless grammatical indiscretions. After practicing this critical reading all day, when they try to write themselves they can't make their grown-up shut up. Publishing companies are full of folks who became editors because they love to read and think of themselves as potential writers. With all their skill, industry contacts, and love of books, you'd think they'd take over the writing field; but they have shamed Bart so many times he refuses to come out of his room. Editors who become writers have overcome a huge obstacle the rest of us will never fully appreciate.

Sometimes you must fool Klink to keep him in the closet. He loves rules, so give him rules: "I can't re-read anything I've written until I've filled five pages with words, any words" or "Write the worst paragraph you can" or "I must write three pages every day, even if they're bad." The best rules are the ones that tell Bart to make a mess. "You must write words for the next two minutes, without stopping, and you can't read any of it until you're done." Your creative genius will squeal with delight, dump finger paints all over the carpet, and throw mud on the walls; but Colonel Klink's happy because you followed the rules. If no words bubble forth from you, you're trying too hard. You're still trying to write well.

Bart and Klink take turns. First, Colonel Klink closets himself while mud erupts from Bart, your secret genius. Wisecracks, absurd analogies, extravagent language, outrageous descriptions and wild plots fly around the room like water balloons filled with mud and paint and ripe tomatos. Sentences are in the wrong order, punctuation screams for editing, easy words misspell themselves. Impossible things happen. Bart is delighted but exhausted.

Then Bart naps while Klink, the grown-up rational editor, sculpts the mud, fixes sentences, corrects spelling, tightens the story, replaces words, and improves the impact.

Don't show your first draft to anyone. It is a muddy mess, not fit for company, with tomato juice dripping from every sentence. If someone reads it and praises the mud on your walls, you'll think you've got a mud-slinging child prodigy within you and you'll skimp on the necessary sculpting. If they criticize, no matter how gently, Bart hears them. Throwing mud will lose its charm; he gets his feelings hurt very easily.

Resist the powerful temptation to share your immortal words prematurely. Just churn out horrible, awkward sentences as fast as you can. A day or two later, let your grownup self read them and make improvements.

Over time, something remarkable will happen. Your first drafts will improve without becoming any less fun. And your revisions will also improve. After you've written something, let it age in a drawer, then revise it, *then* other people can read it. Just don't dwell too much on either their praise or their suggestions. Try to imagine they're giving you advice on something you don't care about, like aluminum siding or taxes. No matter how you prepare, criticism will sting and praise will over-inflate your pride. You don't believe me now, but you've been warned.

The child within you (your muse) has something unique and interesting to say. Give him permission to play unfettered by rules or standards and his voice will emerge. Don't criticize or instruct him. Just let him play. Write whatever comes into your head, and if you find that you're correcting as you write, poke Klink back into the closet with a broom handle. No one can speak for that child or make him speak. Just get out of his way and he'll start chattering.

Because I can't help you with that, most of the rest of this book will be directed at the grown-up. It's about sculpting the mess you make.

But this chapter is the most important. You can't improve without practice, and practice means writing. But you can't write if you won't let yourself. So I'll repeat the message one more time: give yourself permission to write badly.

Write What You Feel

Years ago, I attended a writing conference as a student. During that week each student got to spend a half hour one-on-one with one of the distinguished teachers. My mentor was George Garrett, an excellent writer and teacher who is something of a celebrity in literary circles with dozens of books in print and many awards. By the time we met alone, I'd spent hours in his "critique group" so he was familiar with the writing sample I'd brought.

We began our private session with small talk and the conversation drifted to various other celebrity writers he knew. It would have been a delightful conversation for a cocktail party, because George is a wonderful storyteller with unlimited stories to tell. But I wanted to talk about writing, and we didn't have much time. After several minutes of our precious half hour had ticked away, I realized that this small talk was exactly what many attendees probably wanted. They could chat with a celebrity writer as if they were old friends then go home and repeat the stories, feeling included in that inner circle of successful writers. George understood this and gave them what they wanted.

But that's not why I attended. I interrupted him, probably rudely, and said, "George, how can I improve my writing?"

Instantly his demeanor changed. He leaned forward, not at all insulted or even surprised, and smiled. He had been waiting for the question, which many students probably never ask. If they just wanted to chat he was happy to do that. Now, suddenly, he was all business.

"Kenn," he said, and I was surprised at his instant intensity, "you write good sentences. But there's no emotion in them."

I sat back in my chair, gut-punched by his directness, part of me wanting to argue. Of course there's emotion in my writing. But I resisted. He had given the matter careful thought and developed a strong opinion. He went on to enumerate a multitude of other weakness in my writing. When our time was up, I thanked him, picked up my whimpering inner child, and left.

His other comments concerned technical flaws I could fix. But how do you respond when someone says your writing lacks emotion? Driving home I couldn't get it out of my head. I hoped he was wrong, but what if he wasn't? Why would I have such a flaw, how could I recognize it, and most important, what could I do to correct it?

I decided that maybe my internal editor escaped the closet too soon and made me cautious. Maybe I imagined someone reading my words over my shoulder. If my main character was attracted to a woman who bore no resemblance to my wife, would that hurt my wife's feelings? Better to temper the character's feelings. If I wrote an evil motive, would my sons think I endorsed it? Would my friend see himself in a character and be upset?

What I mostly thought was that George, brilliant writer though he might be, was a lunatic. Dead wrong. I didn't direct my writing to specific readers. Being a scientist at heart, I determined to perform an experiment to prove his mistake. I would pick something I felt strongly about, something deeply personal, and write one page describing exactly how I felt. When I was done I would read it through one time, notice anything interesting, then burn the page in the barbecue grill. Would I write differently if I absolutely knew for certain that no other human would ever read it? I found some matches, waited until I knew no one else would be around, then wrote my page.

To my immense surprise, the page was substantially different in tone from anything I'd ever written. I was even tempted to save it, or at least some of the sentences. Their directness, clarity, and honesty seemed a huge improvement. Sadly, I decided that rules are rules. If I changed my own rules my little mudslinger would know it and wouldn't believe my next manipulation. I took the page out to the grill and watched it blacken, curl, and disappear into smoke.

But the lesson remained: You can't transform emotion into art if you're conscious of the reader. Therefore, write the first draft as if no one will ever read it. When you revise, delete whatever's embarrassing, corny, graphic, or unnecessarily angry before anyone reads it. Emotions are the force that drives fine writing of any kind, but Colonel Klink pounds on the closet door every time you try to access them.

One of two bad things happens when you let someone read a first draft: they like it or they don't.

Praise erodes your motivation to improve. A reader's response is your reward for writing; why revise if you've already received your reward? Praise also undermines your own quality-meter. You thought a sentence was weak, but Mom loved it, so you must be wrong. Why try to improve if everyone says you're already great?

But criticism is just as bad. When criticized, your mudslinger will sulk and refuse to sling more mud. I'll show them, he says. I just won't write anymore and they can't make me.

Criticism skews your quality-meter just like praise does. You thought you wrote a great phrase, but your teacher hates it. Now what do you do? Trust your instincts or get the good grade? Either way, you'll become less adventurous. Too wary of a reader's reactions, you'll become timid.

Cautious writing is boring. It sounds like the homogenous product of a few university creative writing programs. After years of sharp critique, in self defense, their students learn to write sentences that no one can pick apart. Unfortunately, no one wants to read timid, bland writing so those graduates are doomed to careers of teaching creative writing. Some of those programs never produce successful writers but spawn generation after generation of cautious yet overly critical teachers whose own dull writing doesn't sell. Without the teaching income and grants, they'd starve.

Many professors are excellent writers; some have sacrificed writing careers to help others. But before you enroll in a creative writing program, read something written by the instructors. If you don't like it, why would you want them to teach you?

I still write an occasional page for the barbecue grill, and no one reads my first drafts. My family and friends accept this as just one of my many quirks and they no longer even ask. Your family and friends will accept it too.

Big Emotions

There's a dinosaur in your brain, a remnant of our distant ancestors who hunted saber-toothed tigers and wooly mammoths long before editors were invented. When you become angry, terrified, or depressed, this beast takes over your brain and your adult-self (including your internal editor/Colonel Klink/civilized side) hides in the basement. The dinosaur is in charge of big emotions, and while he's on a rampage, you can't access your logical verbal facilities effectively. You lose your debating skills, you forget how sentences fit together, your vocabulary shrinks. You can't verbalize how you feel, and losing that skill may exacerbate the emotions. You say things like, "Words can't express how I feel" or "Why did this happen to me?" or "You talkin' to me, dumbo?" Our dinosaur was useful when the job at hand was running from an angry wooly mammoth, but it never learned to communicate with the parts of our brain that invented tax codes, the Internet, or dictionaries.

The dinosaur lurks within you, sleeping harmlessly, until your parent dies, or you win the Powerball lottery, or you have a child. Then, suddenly, big emotions take over. Your normal methods of managing your life no longer work. You sing in the street, or sob in the basement. You feel out of control.

When you write, you harness the power of those big emotions, transforming them into something positive. Sure, your sentences will be clumsy, your paragraphs won't make sense, and you know as you write that you're making a big mess for someone to fix. But Bart Simpson understands the dinosaur. Gradually, he calms it down. When the beast goes back to sleep, you'll be glad you wrote. The process of revising your words helps process the emotion into something you can file away in organized drawers. By letting the dinosaur write and the editor revise, you create a means for the two parts of your brain to communicate with each other. Sometimes this writing is the most powerful material you'll ever produce. For all the damage he does, the dinosaur always banishes your grown-up self and gives the mudslinger free reign to ride along as he tears up the jungle.

Some people become so accustomed to dealing with emotions by being creative they need it like medicine. While they're creating, the dinosaur is appeased and the artist's emotions remain at a manageable level. If they aren't creative for a period of time, the beast becomes restless; the artist gets depressed or angry. If you're like this, the solution is to write every day. Van Gogh might have saved his ear by painting another field of sunflowers.

In *High Tide in Tucson*, Barbara Kingsolver describes the unique way writing touches reality:

> It's a curious risk, fiction. Some writers choose fantasy as an approach to truth, a way of burrowing under newsprint and formal portraits to find the despair that can stow away in a happy childhood, or the affluent grace of a grandfather in his undershirt. In the final accounting, a hundred different truths are likely to reside at any given address. The part of my soul that is driven to make stories is a fierce thing, like a ferret: long, sleek, incapable of sleep, it digs and bites through all I know of the world. Given that I cannot look away from the painful things, it seems better to invent allegory than to point a straight, bony finger like Scrooge's mute Ghost of Christmas Yet to Come, by declaring, "Here you will end, if you don't clean up your act." By inventing character and circumstance, I like to think I can be a kinder

sort of ghost, saying, "I don't mean you, exactly, but just give it some thought, anyway."

It only makes sense that an author's big emotions will spill onto the page in some fashion once he allows them to. Readers sense this and resonate with them like harp strings tuned to the same pitch: strike one and the other vibrates in sympathy. By using writing to process your own big emotions you get a double whammy benefit: they are diluted within you and sometimes inspire excellent writing.

Five hundred years ago, some poor broken-hearted songwriter wrote "Alas, my love you do me wrong...Greensleeves was my heart of gold..." and we still feel his pain today. When Juliet cries out to Romeo, we feel what Shakespeare surely felt about someone, sometime in his life.

When you see a reader crying over a book, there's a good chance some author was crying while she wrote it.

If you're smiling when you write, that smile may appear on a thousand readers' faces next month and next year and a hundred years from now.

Creativity

Some people can't make their muse shut up. Ideas for stories bubble out of them. Unique and bizarre phrases spring at them like monkeys from trees. Piles of socks suggest alien worlds. Clouds conjure ancient kingdoms. If they drink a glass of tomato juice they imagine themselves a vampire.

These people aren't much different from you and I, they've just practiced letting their inner mudslinger loose. We may never become Stephen King or Frank Herbert or Tom Robbins, but we can become less diligent sergeants of our little recruit. Simply decide to get out of his way, then practice doing so. If the process doesn't seem fun you may decide to create little games to remind you.

Some writers use the "what if?" game. Connie Willis said, "What if I could travel backward in time?" Then she picked some specific place and time and imagined what she might do and what the consequences might be. Her book *To Say Nothing of the Dog* was charming and funny. Others, answering the same "what if" question created dark and disturbing works. Tom Robbins said, "What if my main characters were a spoon and a can?" Stephen King said, "What if someone could start fires with her mind?" Much science fiction starts from a "what if" question. How would civilization be different if apes ruled the world and men were treated like animals? What if vampires lived among us? What if a few humans became immortal?

There are no rules to the "what if" game. Just take a sheet of paper and make a list. Write "what if ... " and then finish the sentence with whatever pops into your mind. Then do it again, trying to fill the page with questions. If you find yourself editing, saying things like, "That's too weird," you're trying too hard. The idea is to make a long list, not a good list.

When you've filled the page, select one of your "what if's" at random and write a paragraph that assumes it's true. Then try another.

The goal of the game isn't to create excellent writing but to notice how if feels to play as you write. It's like learning to ride a bike. At first you're awkward and tentative and feel foolish. At some point you realize Dad isn't holding the handlebars any more and you're pedaling on your own. It feels like flying. Then, of course, you fall down. But as you pick up the bike and brush yourself off, you remember that feeling and know you can do it again. Soon it becomes second nature to you.

Notice that there is no mandatory course in bike riding even though it takes practice and a few skinned knees to learn. Yet seven-year-olds eagerly climb onto their bikes. Trust me, writing is even more fun than riding a bike. You just have to climb on, awaken your muse (perhaps by playing "what if?") and then hold on.

Orson Scott Card describes the awakening of his own muse in the introduction to the 1991 edition of his hugely successful book *Enders Game:*

The novelet "Ender's Game" was my first published science fiction. It was based on an idea—the battle room—that came to me when I was sixteen years old. I had just read Isaac Asimov's Foundation trilogy, which was (more or less) an extrapolation of the ideas in Gibbon's Decline and Fall of the Roman Empire, applied to a galaxy-wide empire in some far future time.

The novel set me, not to dreaming, but to thinking, which is Asimov's most extraordinary ability as a fiction writer. What would the future be like? How would things change? What would remain the same?...

So one morning, as my Dad drove me to Brigham Young High School along Carterville Road in the heavily wooded bottoms of the Provo River, I wondered: How would you train soldiers for combat in the future? ... The result of my speculations that morning was the Battle Room, exactly as you will see it ... in this book.

One "what if" question launched his career.

Another trick is to try making connections between seemingly unrelated concepts. How is a chair like a bird? How is music similar to fire? What's the relationship between the color red and building a house? The answers don't come from your serious adult brain, they come from a muddy urchin you've kept in the basement for too long. That's the part of yourself you want to exercise.

Make lists of things that have no apparent relationship, then try to create sentences that link them in some way. If the two concepts are music and fire, you might come up with:

"The guitarist began his solo slowly, his fingers moving across the strings as if they were twigs he rubbed together. Notes rose like smoke, overtones sparked from the strings. Soon his fingers moved too quickly to see, and arpeggios and chords blazed in the night. The crowd leaned forward to bask in their heat."

Something like that. Is music like fire? Not really, not to a grown up. But when you're just playing, any two concepts can be related. Some you'll like, some you'll laugh at. Doesn't matter. Practice playing.

Another way to get started writing is just to look around you and write what you see, or remember something that interested you and write about that. Here's a paragraph by E.B. White in an essay "A Report in Spring," written in 1957. He's just returned to the city after spending time in the country and simply remembers it:

> One never knows what images one is going to hold in memory, returning to the city after a brief orgy in the country. I find this morning that what I most vividly and longingly recall is the sight of my grandson and his little sunburnt sister returning to their kitchen door from an excursion, with trophies of the meadow clutched in their hands—she with a couple of violets, and smiling, he serious and holding dandelions, strangling them in a responsible grip. Children hold spring so tightly in their brown fists—just as grown-ups, who are less sure of it, hold it in their hearts.

He writes down what he remembers, as if writing a letter: this is how my summer vacation went. You can do that, too: this is what happened on my commute to work this morning, this is the dream I had last night.

Many writing classes provide weird exercises to inspire you. Take two completely different paragraphs by writers you admire and write your own paragraph to join them. Make up strange rules, like some types of poetry have: every sentence must have so many syllables or rhyme a certain way or start with certain letters. Write two pages without ever stopping to think about what you're writing. Imagine you are some inanimate object, like the murder weapon, and write the murder scene from that perspective. The idea of all of these is to distract you away from the work at hand. It's like observing a faint star – sometimes you can only see it if you don't look directly at it. If your internal mudslinger requires this kind of persuasion, by all means belt him with it. On the other hand, if you have given him permission to write badly, to play, to smear mud on the new couch, you may not need to do more.

Thinking about Language

First drafts represent a world without boundaries. Anything is possible. No need to restrict yourself in any way. Forget making sense or using good grammar. Spelling is irrelevant. Each word can be fixed, or not fixed, or eliminated when you go back to revise. No one will ever see it anyway. Remember, you are playing with mud, and that's a game without rules.

Revising isn't a process of "trying to get it correct." Correct is a meaningless word in the world of art. Revising means making choices. Which rules or conventions do you want to adopt? Will you leave in this thing or take it out? Will you move this section or not? Do you choose to replace this word or sentence with a fresher one?

Before you begin writing, you have only a foggy idea about potential choices. After you've created a first draft, every word you've written becomes a choice to make: keep it, replace it, or remove it.

People talk about a writer's "voice." After reading one of my books, people often say, "Kenn, I could sure hear you speaking in that book. It sounded just like you." I cautiously accept that as some sort of compliment because people like to connect with a writer, to become friends on some level. They want each writer to seem unique and recognizable. A writer's "voice" isn't revealed by the first words that come into his head, but by the choices he makes to improve them later. If a dozen competent writers rewrote the same first draft, they'd arrive at twelve completely different finished products. If a dozen less-experienced writers took on the same task, the final products would all sound about the same.

The next sections will illustrate the kinds of decisions you can make while revising. I'll give examples from well-known writers to illustrate the choices they made. If you like some of them, you may decide to make similar choices. If you dislike others, don't copy them.

I'm not going to tell you the right way to write; there is no such beast. We just make different choices.

Vocabulary

Avid readers see many new words; it's how we build our vocabularies. Eventually we infer their meanings and start using them, but it doesn't hurt to have a dictionary handy. Sometimes I think I understand a word I've read many times and my arrogance gets me in trouble.

For one thing, one can guess wrong about pronunciation. I still remember learning the word "horizon" as a child. I gradually deduced its meaning but I'd never heard the word spoken. Then I read *David and the Phoenix* by Edward Ormondroyd. In one section, David and his benevolent but pompous friend the Phoenix are riding on the back of a sea monster as they search for buried treasure:

> The Sea Monster was a magnificent swimmer. Its neck cut through the water like the stem of Viking ship, and it left a frothing wake behind. Every once in a while it would plunge its head into the water and come up with a fish, which it would swallow whole.
>
> "Would you like some breakfast, David?" said the Sea Monster.
>
> "No, thank you," David answered, "but you go right ahead. Phoenix," he added, "what are you doing?"
>
> The Phoenix, which had been walking up and down with its wings clasped behind its back, stopped and gazed over the sea. "Pacing the quarter-deck, my boy. Scanning the horizon. That is what one usually does at sea, I believe."
>
> "You'll be wanting us to call you Admiral next," said the Sea Monster acidly.

For days I marched around the living room repeating the phrase "pacing the quarter deck, scanning the horizon." Only I pronounced it "HOR- eh-zohn." My parents thought it quite amusing. Of historical interest, that book provided some of my best elementary school comedy material, like "The feline's existence was terminated as a direct result of its inquisitiveness." It also inspired me to become a writer.

Sometimes you'll infer an incorrect meaning. After seeing "miasma" a number of times, I was sure it meant a lovely fog. What a beautiful word, I thought, with a glorious meaning. I used it whenever I could. Only it really means a putrid swamp gas. Wise writers use words they're absolutely sure of.

Words are a writer's tools, and using the best tool for any job improves your craftsmanship. The more words you know, the better your odds of picking the most precise one.

But the world is full of folks who don't read as much as you do and therefore don't know as many words. If you're an enthusiastic reader, you've already learned to dumb down your everyday speaking vocabulary, perhaps without even noticing. As children we learned that bullies think we're ridiculing them when we use big words. The cute guys on the junior high football team are threatened by smart girls. We don't want to get beat up or rejected, so we keep most of our vocabulary back at home in the dresser drawer. We adopt a universal, common-denominator vocabulary and eschew words like "eschew."

You'll be delighted to learn that you don't need to restrict yourself like that when you write. Think about it: you're communicating with other people who like to read, and they know all the same words you do. Writers tend to seek out new words like little treasures. We have an exclusive club with a secret language not available to outsiders. The language is English, but all of English, not just subway/shopping mall English. You can use that to your advantage, because your reader knows more words than most of your characters do. The way characters use words, and react to words, helps define them. Here's an example from *I Hear America Swinging*, by Peter DeVries:

> "I know. Like ceiling murals and friezes everywhere, even the walls of the washrooms. Parallels with the Roman Empire and all that. Emphasis on bathrooms. That's what the doomsters say."
>
> Luke shifted his weight a little against the fender,

at the same time folding his arms. "Can't see for the life of me why there shouldn't be friezes in bathrooms. After all they're made for relief."

So this gazebo was bi-lingual. He could talk United States, or he could bandy brittle dialogue with the best of them, shifting gears effortlessly from one to the other depending on whether he had to pull the wool over your eyes or the rug out from under you.

We learn about Luke by the way he makes the weird pun, and learn about the narrator by the way he notices it, understands it, and uses it to define Luke in his mind. His own internal language, full of quirky metaphors and invented terms, defines him to us as well. He calls the guy a gazebo, creates a new definition of bilingual, and throws in a driving metaphor and twisted versions of two clichés to boot. This is a busy writer who assumes his readers will keep up.

One pleasure of hanging out with other writers is the magnificent smorgasbord of words they know. When they assemble, you sense their great relief at not having to confine themselves to the words even children know. You can't shut them up. Most writing books don't mention this benefit: you belong to a family that loves words the way you do, and you'll find each other when you start to write.

All the ten dollar words arrive with nuances and history that augment their meanings, color their power, and invoke images. This is both good and bad. You gain extra meaning without spending additional words if you use them well, but you sound dumb if you use them badly. No one had heard the word "vetting" much before the O.J. Simpson trial was televised and prospective jurors had to be "vetted." We all figured out that it meant they had to be screened and approved, so it entered common usage. In the 1800s the word meant taking an animal to a veterinarian to have its health checked out before you bought it. If you know that, the word carries with it an extra faint flavor from its past. Checking references says one thing; vetting an employee implies taking him to the veterinarian like you would a mule, to make sure he doesn't have rabies. Vetting a potential girlfriend sounds a little odd in that context, doesn't it? This paragraph from *Skinny Legs and All* by Tom Robbins uses many words and images that are ripe with contextual meanings:

> In cries or whispers, depending upon their style, the public journals told of curfews and roadblocks, flaming tires and bulldozed kitchens, bridal veils of tear gas and sweaters of blood; told of leaders with tongues of stale lightning, cradles filled with stones, and young girls who danced with live ammunition when they should have been dancing with their fathers (too young to dance with boys); told of the old primate grab-and-hold—the berserk baboon dance that anthropologists call "territorial imperative" and politicians call "national interest"; told of the gash that four thousand years had not sewn shut, the lunatic legacy of Isaac and Ishmael.

That's dark and vivid writing if you understand the history of his terms. The paragraph is about the Middle East, probably Israel, although it is never mentioned specifically. Terrorists often blocked roads by piling up tires and lighting them on fire. Protesters hid rocks in cradles and baby carriages to throw at the police, the police struck back with tear gas, sometimes too aggressively, and many civilians died. Territorial imperative, a term from science, is the subject of many books. Using it conjures up the memory of lively debates about the subject and implies the behavior of primitive animals. Both Isaac and Ishmael were sons of Abraham. According to tradition, the descendents of Isaac became the Jewish people, while the descendents of Ishmael became Arabs. These groups have been quarreling and fighting for centuries despite their common ancestor. Knowing that context gives the passage impact for a reader. In fact, one can't really grasp the writer's intent at all without it. For those who know the terms, this is fabulous shorthand; my explanation is longer than the original paragraph. For those who don't, it's just confusing. Try reading it again and see if it seems richer.

45

If you use a word you're not sure of, you risk spinning unintended meanings. The word "metamorphosis" suggests caterpillars changing to butterflies. If you only know the literal meaning of change, you might use it in an odd way. "He gave the storekeeper a ten dollar bill and asked him for metamorphosis."

Usually it's subtle. Burgeoning comes from biology and means growing rapidly, a plant budding and sprouting a new leaf, the exuberant explosion of new life. If you say the pile of newspapers burgeoned, you've created a weird image in the reader's mind. It's not wrong, but picturing the pile of newspapers as a living thing requires a mental stretch. "The rumor burgeoned" paints an image of gossip developing a life of its own and growing like a jungle vine, which somehow feels right.

If you're not comfortable with a word, use it carefully. Imprecise gratuitous sesquipedalians obfuscate. The burgeoning miasma they promulgate sounds contrived and pretentious.

Big Screen, Small Screen

In the 20th century, a new form of literature swept the world: movies. People gathered together in auditoriums to watch images move across a huge screen. Playwrights had to adjust their writing to this powerful medium.

In darkened auditoriums, huge images filled our fields of vision. The size of the screen amplified events. When Indiana Jones raised one eyebrow, it moved ten feet on the screen and conveyed all the information the audience needed. He was fed up by being pursued and was about to teach his tormentor a lesson about the folly of bringing a big knife to a gunfight. He didn't need to launch into a speech describing his internal conflict and the audience would have groaned if he tried. The music changed, the bad guy stopped, eyes wide, as he understood his goose was about to get cooked. The audience leaned forward, the youngsters cheered. The writing could be understated; we all saw what was going on. In fact, the writing *had* to be understated. With the bright colors, huge movements, and loud music, a lot of fancy words would be excess hot sauce on a spicy dish or a weird metaphor when we already got the point. Just let Indiana raise one eyebrow on that huge screen and we all understood.

But when the same movie plays on television, Indiana's eyebrow only rises a quarter of an inch. From across the room, we might not even notice it. We do not lean forward in our chairs, no one cheers. We wonder why we thought the movie so compelling the first time we saw it. The understated writing, no longer augmented by huge movements and loud music, pales.

The folks who produce television shows compensate for this smaller screen by exaggeration. Actors talk louder than life and gesture more extravagantly. Their jokes are less subtle. TV producers may even add the sound of an audience laughing to reinforce the idea that we've just witnessed something funny. No one adds laugh tracks to big-screen movies; they don't have to. Television dramas often include backgrounds of unnaturally vivid colors or have characters wear clothes that would seem garishly over-stated in real life. The audience at home doesn't even notice. These shows actually seem more realistic to us because the exaggeration helps our imaginations compensate for the small screen.

Words on a page inhabit an even smaller screen. They don't have the benefit of colors, movement, sound, music, or laugh tracks. The page fills a tiny part of our field of vision. The scene is filtered first through the writer's mind to the page, then through the reader's eyes, mind, and imagination. The story must compete with distracting activity and sounds surrounding the reader.

To survive the dimming effect of all that filtering when projected onto such a small screen, writers compensate by crafting images that are more vivid than reality. One way is simply exaggerating. When taken to an extreme, this can have a comic effect. If Dave Barry says that someone's nose is the size of Montana, we smile, but we don't stop reading. We just picture an unusually large nose. If Annie Dillard says someone's nose is the size and color of a ripe plum, we get a vivid image, despite the fact that the nose in question is probably actually smaller and less plum-colored than her description. After all the filtering, on the small screen of the page, the image comes through about right.

To pump up their language, writers use many tools. Simple exaggeration is one. Choosing active verbs over passive verbs is another (passive verbs include is, was, were, be etc. We'll talk more about them later.) Attributing characteristics of animals or humans to inanimate objects is another. Choosing vivid nouns is another. We all recognize exaggeration in daily life, but in the written word, remarkably, after being filtered by the page, it does not leap out at us the way you'd expect it would.

Here's a section from *Tale of the Body Thief* by Anne Rice describing the rain forest of South America. Does it seems bold enough, or is it too exaggerated for your taste?

Birds with feathers the color of the summer sky or the burning sun streak through the wet branches. Monkeys scream as they reach out with their tiny clever little hands for vines as thick as hemp rope. Sleek and sinister mammals of a thousand shapes and sizes crawl in remorseless search of one another over monstrous roots and half-buried saplings dying in the fetid darkness, even as they suck their last nourishment from the reeking soil.

Mindless and endlessly vigorous is the cycle of hunger and satiation, of violent and painful death. Reptiles with eyes as hard and shining as opals feast eternally upon the writhing universe of still and crackling insects as they have since the days when no warm-blooded creature ever walked the earth. And the insects—winged, fanged, pumped with deadly venom, and dazzling in their hideousness and ghastly beauty, and beyond all cunning—ultimately feast upon all.

There is no mercy in this forest. No mercy, no justice, nor worshipful appreciation of its beauty, no soft cry of joy at the beauty of the falling rain. Even the sagacious little monkey is a moral idiot at heart.

Are the birds really the color of the burning sky? Are the reptile eyes really as hard as opals? Are the monkey hands really clever? Probably not, yet when filtered through the words the images don't seem outlandish but merely vivid. Anne chooses seven active verbs compared to three passive ones, and the active ones are bold as pirates: birds *streak*, monkeys *scream*, mammals *crawl*, reptiles *feast*, roots *suck*. She pulls adjectives from the top drawer as well. Nothing is "big" when it can be "monstrous." The universe isn't active, it's writhing. The darkness doesn't just smell, it's fetid. Beauty is ghastly, monkeys are sagacious, and even their hands are clever. Does her writing seem "over the top" to you? Fine, then don't write like her. But if you found yourself transported to a magical and dangerous jungle within three paragraphs, notice how she did it. You can do that, too.

Compare that with a description of jungle and desert in *Nature* by the Encyclopedia of Nature. This is a lovely little book written for children, so its language is perfectly appropriate for the job:

> A desert and a rain forest have similar air temperatures, but lush vegetation can only grow in the rainforest because the air is very moist, or humid. The heat of the desert, however, is very dry. This lack of moisture means that few plants can survive.

This example contains the three gentle active verbs "have," "grow", and "means" and two passive verbs. These timid verbs don't propel us into the undergrowth, but they provide information for the reader. We don't want to scare the kids and this description feels safe. Not exciting, but safe. If that's the tone you seek, don't exaggerate.

Once I tried an experiment to see how much exaggeration I could get away with. As I wrote one of my books, I consciously exaggerated descriptions as much as I could. The book was supposed to be amusing anyway, so I thought some of this wildness might come across as funny. But I knew that many of the images were too extreme by any standard, that readers would rebel at the outrageous exaggerations. For the fun of it, I left them all in, fully prepared to revise them down to a respectable size later. Before I did, I let about a dozen people read the book.

Predictably, each reader found things to complain about. They questioned my character's motives, complained about elements of the plot, and disagreed with the ending. Astonishingly, not one reader even noticed the outrageous exaggeration. Playing on the small screen, the images simply seemed vivid, or at least mildly amusing. In fact, that was the one universal compliment I received — people liked my descriptions. Here is an example from that book, *The Land of Debris and the Home of Alfredo:*

> I did not remember other showers, but this one felt good. Better than good. It was a hot and soapy heaven of a shower. A steaming ecstasy. A mystical, cathartic, soul-liberating symphony of cleansing, massaging droplets caressing every inch of my body like a million tiny geishas.

As I wrote that I thought: this is doomed writing. I will become the butt of every Colorado writer's jokes for the rest of my life. This is so over-the-top, even for humor, that everyone who reads it will cross it out with a red pen and make an eloquently insulting remark in the margin. I prepared for humiliation and left it in.

No one said a thing. No one noticed.

This small-screen effect spills into other aspects of writing as well. Small conflicts, vague emotions and tentative actions rarely survive on the printed page. Most mysteries involve a murder; smaller crimes fade to insignificance in the hands of any but the most skilled craftsmen. A perfect description of an ordinary life, with its daily challenges and decisions, shrinks to triviality. I don't pick up a book to live a life that's even more boring than my own.

It's easy to watch movies and television. We forgive dull dialog if a pretty actress speaks it, and tap our feet to the driving sound track even if we've seen this car chase scene a hundred times. But when we read, every word demands an instant of attention. Readers will invest that effort only to the extent that their reward exceeds it. Exaggeration is one way to give them more value for their investment. Writing endless strings of brilliant sentences is another. But writing brilliant sentences is a chore.

Be Concise

For most of us, the easiest strategy for maintaining the effort/reward balance is to eliminate unnecessary words. For the same reader reward, efficient sentences require less reader effort. This culling of extra words consumes re-writing time, but it's worth it. Just consider how we might have written the previous sentence: "You will find that taking a lot of time locating extra words and then rewriting the sentences that contain them with an eye to trimming out any unnecessary words and replacing them with more concise and vivid words and phrases will decrease your reader's effort in reading them, while conveying all the same information you intended in the first place, which is the reader's reward."

Sentences like that remind me why I never let anyone read my first drafts. Here's how it might work:

First Draft:
    A secret pact exists between readers and writers. Readers spend their *time* to purchase information or entertainment, or both. Writers spend *words* to buy praise, immortality, adulation and money. Each extra word costs the reader time. If it does not increase her benefit, she will soon move on to a writer she perceives as a better bargain. This will cost the writer praise, immortality, adulation, and money.

Second Draft:
Don't send ten words to do the job of two.

Third Draft:
Be brief.

Does each draft say exactly the same thing? Clearly not. In some situations might one choose the more elaborate first draft? Certainly. But if the idea was that our hero made some toast before something important happened, we might question spending two hundred words on the brand of toaster, the pedigree of the marmalade, and the price of the bread. Sometimes the best way to express what we need expressed is, "John was making toast when the bullet hit him."

Active and Passive Verbs

Verbs drive sentences the way a locomotive pulls the rest of the train. Choose powerful verbs to pull your sentences.

Verbs come in two varieties: active and passive. Passive verbs include all variations of the verb "to be" and convey a thing's state or condition. The most common passive verbs are: be, is, was, were, are, been, and am. Other words that describe a condition include have, had, has etc. Although they indicate that one thing possesses something else, possessing isn't very active. He *has* red hair. He *had* a dream.

Textbook writers love passive verbs. Passive verbs remove the writer from the sentence and make it sound less personal and more official. Maybe textbook writers think passive sentences make them sound smarter. If you want your work to sound like a bad, boring textbook, stick to passive verbs. They're easy to write.

Passive verbs describe conditions: the chair *is* red. Active verbs describe activities and, generally speaking, activites are more interestng than conditions. Active verbs communicate with more precision, more power, and more originality than passive verbs. If you want your words to leap from the page, replace about half the passive verbs with active ones. You can replace "The job of verbs is to drive sentences" with "Verbs drive sentences." No new words; we just identified the activity of the sentence and used that as the verb. "He was sitting in the chair" becomes "He sat in the chair." Same idea, we just eliminated the passive verb. Your instincts will whisper to ignore crazy Kenn, that your idea cannot be expressed without "is" or "are." Sometimes that's true, and we all employ passive verbs, but it's true less often than your instincts suggest. After all my preaching about passive verbs, Scott Amdahl (yes, he's related) wrote a complete novel without a single passive verb and it didn't suffer from it. It just seemed lively. Most readers don't notice active verbs because they become engrossed in the story. They don't notice passive verbs either because, after a page or two, they're too sleepy to notice anything.

Use passive verbs when they are the most concise way to express something, when no powerful verb seems natural, or when you just can't think of one. The goal is simplicity and clarity, and sometimes the simplest, clearest solution involves the verb "to be." But passive verbs in unclear sentences weaken your writing in two ways: they confuse and bore us at the same time.

Here's a really fun game: rate the dullness of your own work by counting the passive verbs on your average page. Compare your average with a writer you admire. If they use 50 percent passive verbs and you use 95 percent, draw your own conclusions.

Passive verbs are uniformly drab. He is something, he was something, he will be something. The strongest adjective can't compete with a good verb. "He was unsure about the decision" pales next to "He anguished over the decision." Passive verbs remain seated, observing the party but never quite participating.

Active verbs dance many dances, from the tame to the wild. By choosing from them you orchestrate the mood of the party. The more vivid and precise your verb, the livelier your sentence. "He sat in the chair" may be accurate, but "He slumped in the chair" conveys more information and a more vivid image in the same number of words. Perhaps your character perches on the chair, or engulfs the chair, or relaxes, reclines, holds court, or reigns from his chair. Why spend an extra sentence conveying information that one well-chosen verb can convey? Why sit with the wall flowers when you can leap and laugh at the center of the dance floor?

A man *was* walking down the street.

No points will be deducted from your story for that sentence. But your grade will improve slightly with:

A man *walked* down the street.

It's shorter (and therefore more efficient) and we eliminated the passive verb. But "walked" is a ten-cent word, imprecise and dull.

A man *staggered* down the street.

Now your reader perks up. For the same reading effort he enjoys a more vivid image plus he learns more information. The character is either injured or drunk.

Verbs range from dull and vague passive verbs to raging, leaping, swashbuckling verbs that ensnare your reader, hypnotize him, and finally eviscerate his emotions. Select them according to the task at hand. If you merely want to hold your reader's hand while he drifts casually though your sentences, pleasant little verbs can get the job done. If you want to reach out from the page, clutch the reader's throat, and wrench him into your world, choose swashbuckling verbs.

A side benefit is that your own unique voice arises from your choice of verbs. You might write ten books without choosing the verb "eviscerate," while I might summon it three times in one chapter. Your own vocabulary, personality, taste, and style shine through your verbs. On the other hand, passive verbs effectively conceal their author. Committee reports always use passive verbs to blend away individual personalities. If you ever write a blackmail note, use passive verbs. The police will never figure out who you are.

Often you'll want to fall somewhere in the middle of the active/passive scale. Too extreme and you risk committing humor. Too passive and no one will be able to slog through your writing. Here's an example of the middle way from *A Walk in the Woods* by Bill Bryson:

> We took off our shoes and socks, rolled up our pants, and stepped gingerly out into the frigid water. The stones on the bottom were all shapes and sizes—flat, egg-shaped, domed—very hard on the feet, and covered with a filmy green slime that was ludicrously slippery. I hadn't gone three steps when my feet skated and I fell painfully on my ass. I struggled halfway to my feet but slipped and fell again; struggled up, staggered sideways a yard or two, and pitched helplessly forward, breaking my fall with my hands and ending up in the water doggie-style.

As I landed, my pack slid forward and my boots, tied to its frame by their laces, were hurled into a kind of contained orbit; they came around the side of the pack in a long, rather pretty trajectory, and came to a halt against my head, then plunked into the water, where they dangled in the current. As I crouched there, breathing evenly and telling myself that one day this would be a memory, two young guys—clones almost of the two we had seen the day before—strode past with confident, splashing steps, packs above their heads.

"Fall down?" one said brightly.

"No, I just wanted to take a closer look at the water." You moronic fit twit.

In that stretch we see only three carefully chosen passive verbs: "The stones *were*..." (If anything in the world deserves passive verbs, it's stones on the bottom of a creek because stones are intrinsically passive.)

The slime *was* ludicrously slippery; "was" is the most efficient verb for the job.

"*Were* hurled" doesn't seem static, despite being technically passive.

The rest of his verbs sparkle: rolled, stepped, struggled, fell, pitched, staggered, slid, dangled, crouched, and strode.

Once you notice where writers fall on the boldness scale, you can aim your own writing at your favorite mark on that scale. Simply count active and passive verbs on a random page in your favorite book. Then count them on one of your pages. Many varieties of writing share muscular verbs driving vivid sentences: dark, disturbing stories and humorous columns; literary masterpieces and goofy letters. On the other hand, some authors attempt to create action and suspense by hitching their wagons to passive verbs. Unfortunately, I don't own any of those books, so I can't give you examples.

How does the next section rate on the active/passive scale? It's by Annie Dillard from *Pilgrim at Tinker Creek*:

That day it was dark inside the cottage, as usual; the five windows framed five films of the light and living world. I crunched to the creekside window, walking on the layer of glass shards on the floor, and stood to watch the creek lurch over the dam and round the shaded bend under the cliff, while bumblebees the size of ponies fumbled in the fragrant flowers that flecked the bank. A young cottontail rabbit bounded into view and froze. It crouched under my window with its ears flattened to its skull and its body motionless, the picture of adaptive invisibility. With one ridiculous exception. It was so very young, and its shoulder itched so maddeningly, that it whapped away at the spot noisily with a violent burst of a hind leg—and then resumed its frozen alert. Over the dam's drop of waters, two dog-faced sulphur butterflies were fighting. They touched and parted, ascending in a vertical climb, as though they were racing up an invisible spiraling vine.

All at once something wonderful happened, although at first it seemed perfectly ordinary. A female goldfinch suddenly hove into view. She lighted weightlessly on the head of a bankside purple thistle and began emptying the seedcase, sowing the air with down.

The lighted frame of my window filled. The down rose and spread in all directions, wafting over the dam's waterfall and wavering between the tulip trunks and into the meadow. It vaulted towards the orchard in a puff; it hovered over the ripening pawpaw fruit and staggered up the steep-faced terrace. It jerked, floated, rolled, veered, swayed. The thistledown faltered toward the cottage and gusted clear to the motorbike woods; it rose and entered the shaggy arms of pecans. At last it strayed like snow, blind and sweet, into the pool of the creek upstream and into the race of the creek over rocks down. It shuddered onto the tips of growing grasses, where it poised, light, still wracked by errant quivers. I was holding my breath. Is this where we live, I thought, in this place at this moment, with the air so light and wild?

I count four passive verbs in that entire passage, compared to 40 active verbs. And these are not mere everyday verbs she found in the sock drawer, these are vivid special-occasion verbs: whapped, staggered, froze, shuddered, gusted, crunched, lurched, jerked, floated, rose, swayed, hovered, faltered, vaulted. To my taste, this writing satisfies. If you prefer, "A bird was eating thistle seeds. It was making a mess. The down was going everywhere," then tailor your writing accordingly and stick with passive verbs.

I'm not suggesting you eliminate passive verbs. Every verb is a choice to make, and each choice changes the character of a work. Different writers make different choices, and a writer will make different choices depending on the task at hand. William Shakespeare wrote: "To be or not to be, that is the question." Perhaps just to spite me, Bill managed to use three passive verbs in that little jewel. His sentence, rather than seeming weak, is revered by writers everywhere because it is the most brilliantly concise and precise way to say what he wanted. In the play, the line is spoken by a depressed and possibly insane character contemplating suicide. Should he live (to be) or die (not to be)? Should he kill himself or not? No alternative expression feels as concise or powerful.

In *Harry Potter and the Sorcerer's Stone*, the first of J.K. Rowling's Harry Potter books, the story opens in the land of humans, a very ordinary place and magic-free. Harry does not know he's a wizard. He lives with dull, unpleasant folks who glory in their ordinariness. As the book begins in this drab world, the author uses passive verbs exclusively:

> Mr. and Mrs. Dursley, of number four, Privet Drive, were proud to say that they were perfectly normal, thank you very much. They were the last people you'd expect to be involved in anything strange or mysterious, because they just didn't hold with such nonsense.

For several pages the book uses nearly all passive verbs. Do you suppose this fabulously successful author simply doesn't know any better than to use only passive verbs? Do you suppose she disagrees with me on this point? Or do you think maybe she wanted to cast a spell of "ordinary and boring" over the Dursleys and knew that passive verbs would do the trick? To find out, we look deeper in the book and see how she uses active and passive verbs.

I checked several pages at random later in the book, when magic has entered. In my unscientific study, on page after random page, she uses half active verbs and half passive. This is a huge leap from the first pages, when she used 100 percent passive verbs, so I'm guessing it's intentional.

On a page with important action I counted four passive verbs versus twenty active ones. Now characters wheel, sprint, knock into, throw, yell and gasp. We're not at the Dursley's any more:

> "Come on, Harry!" Hermione screamed, leaping onto her seat to watch as Harry sped straight at Snape— she didn't even notice Malfoy and Ron rolling around under her seat...
>
> The stands erupted; it had to be a record, no one could remember the Snitch being caught so quickly.

Remember, the first page of this book used passive verbs exclusively; the plain non-magic world could be easily described in beige tones of were, was, and had. Two hundred pages later, in a magical land, the characters snap, clamber, scream, leap, and roll. Objects shoot past, the crowd erupts. Coincidence? You be the judge. Then decide if you want your prose to live at number four Privet Drive or at Hogwarts Castle.

Anyone can write passive-verb sentences and all sound equally dull. But I won't declare them wrong; use them if you like them. If you want to say, "My character was walking down the street," fine. Just don't complain when my character leaps from the shadows to eviscerate him.

Nouns

Now that you've harnessed strong verbs to your sentences, choose precise nouns for them to pull. Nouns are the words that define people, places and things. Vague nouns slow the train because they require more words to clarify them.

"The man stumbled," creates a limited image because the word "man" conveys little information; it only narrows the field to two billion possible people. To convey more than that, you must spend extra words. Or, you could replace the noun "man" with something more specific.

"The president stumbled," is more concentrated. How many presidents can there be? Certainly not two billion. But is it the president of Microsoft or the president of Tunisia?

When you say "Bill Clinton stumbled," a precise image springs into the reader's mind. It conveys much more information than "the man stumbled."

If a man sits beneath a tree, we all know what you mean, in a general way. If a priest sits beneath a blooming apple tree, we know a lot more. Precise nouns focus your writing.

Invisible Words

By incessant repetition, some words have become invisible. Words like "the" and "and" are placeholders and organizers. You don't need to worry about them; they don't cost the reader any effort because he doesn't notice them.

The word "said" falls into this category. In an effort to spice their writing, many beginners substitute more flavorful expressions. Their characters never "say" anything, they remark, respond, cry, complain and cajole. Like any spice, substitutes for "he said" are most effective in moderation. If the character actually screams out the word "stop" then *"Stop!" he screamed* is the most accurate way to describe it. If he screams out one line, then cries the next line, then whispers the next, then complains, your reader will become fascinated by his weird emotions and miss whatever he actually says. Force the reader to focus on the dialog itself. If your character whispers his first line, we assume he's whispering the next ones as well. If he's shouting, we only need to be told once. Don't rely on punctuation to convey emotion, especially exclamation points. Let your words do the work! Repeated exclamation points just seem goofy!

Analogies

People instinctively compare things. When they have trouble explaining a concept, they compare it to something more understandable. Your friend might stare blankly when you suggest that a particular football running back "develops a high degree of inertia supplemented by a continuous application of energy from his ample quadriceps." So you explain it another way. You say, "He runs like a locomotive."

Your friend smiles and nods, "Yes, he's a beast."

The word "locomotive" conveys several images at once because we know a lot about trains. Locomotives are big, strong, and made of hard metal. They crush things in their paths, they're hard to stop once they get up to speed, they're indifferent to small influences. They're also mindless and noisy, belching out smoke as their pistons churn. Their wheels relentlessly follow the track.

Obviously, our running back is no locomotive. He probably doesn't have wheels, for example. But on the small screen of the written word, the comparison works. It works better than a more accurate description because it's efficient: with one word we conjure a dozen characteristics. Analogies are always a way of comparing one thing to something else that is usually not obvious.

Analogies come in four main varieties.

Similes use the words "like" or "as" to make a comparison; for example: "My love is like a rose." The reader must resolve any ambiguity. Do we mean our beloved is thorny and requires lots of attention or that she is beautiful, soft, and romantic? John Dunne built a career writing poetry that compared the lady in question to things like drawing-compasses and fading flowers. It worked for him, because he wrote many words clarifying his position. For guys like you and me, the best similes convey our intent with little amplification. If you say your love is like a hippopotamus, she may not immediately grasp that you admire her ability to hold her breath.

Here's a simile from John McPhee in *Coming Into the Country:*

> People throng to the post office like seagulls around a piling, like trout at the mouth of a brook. Many, of both races, wear sweatshirts and windbreakers on which are stenciled the words "Eagle, Alaska."

A metaphor does not use the words "like" or "as." It's a statement of equivalency: "my love is a rose." Most metaphors are outright lies. Face it, your love isn't a rose. Your attorney isn't a bulldog. If you possess a heightened regard for literal truth, you may squirm at making metaphorical statements. You don't like to lie.

In the writing arena, lying is a job requirement. Smart writers romance the truth all the time; they pump up their images so that, when they filter down to a reader's brain, the truth survives.

People don't talk much about the third kind of analogy and, as far as I know, it doesn't have a name. I call it the implied metaphor.

In an implied metaphor, words associated with one thing describe something else. When you say, "The students blossomed in the new school," you're using an implied metaphor. Students don't actually sprout petals, flowers do. Some sort of analogy is at work, but it's neither a simile nor a metaphor. "The students' minds opened like flowers" would be a simile. "The students' minds were flowers opening in spring" would be a metaphor. Crafty devil that you are, by saying the students blossomed, you're conjuring all the sunflowers in Kansas without spending the words to make an overt comparison. You're letting the reader's mind do that. If your implied metaphor is a good one, the reader won't even notice. He won't feel he's done more work, but less.

Many implied metaphors have become entrenched in our language. Dancers glide across the floor, the sun bakes our backs, sultry women purr. Your reader will purr and glide through these images unoffended, but also not moved to tears. Your writing will begin to sparkle when you pan the streams of your own imagination for implied metaphors that glisten as you melt, mold, and hammer them to your own ring size.

Of course, they won't all work.

Easy metaphors do little damage; they slip past us without impact. Extreme metaphors may stun and astonish us with their appropriateness, or confuse us, or make us laugh. The trick is to summon the right-sized genie for the wish you want granted.

The terms "simile" and "metaphor" don't matter once you pass your grammar test. What's important is noticing whether or not your favorite authors use analogies. If they do, and you like it, use them yourself. Here's a short paragraph from *Skinny Legs and All* by Tom Robbins in which he creates an analogy and extends it for his purposes:

> Early religions were like muddy ponds with lots of foliage. Concealed there, the fish of the soul could splash and feed. Eventually however, religions became aquariums. Then, hatcheries. From farm fingerling to frozen fish stick is a short swim.

Or this one from Garrison Keillor's essay, "The Killer:"

> It's easy for Wally to be a realist. He spends his days in the Sidetrack Tavern like a bear in a cave — a cave with green and orange and blue neon beer signs and a bevy of older bears leaning against the bar and belching beer breath. Wally stands in the dark, listening to the bears grumbling and mumbling, and he doesn't know much about how the lovely world outside can raise our hopes.

Obviously, there are no actual bears in the bar. But we understand the image.

A specific kind of analogy suggests that animals or things have human characteristics. This is called anthropomorphosis, a word that may win a word game for you some day.

See if you can spot any examples of analogies in the next example. Similes? Metaphors? Implied metaphor? Anthropomorphosisms?

This from George Garrett's book, *The King of Babylon shall not Come Against You:*

> Quincy County is long and narrow and flat as can be. The northern part is much more like south Georgia or Alabama than the name and image of Florida might invoke. Wide acres of green and shadowy pine woods (with, here and there, some live oaks and post oaks and blackjack oaks with their beards and wigs of Spanish moss), woods orchestrated by insects, haunted by birdsong, brooded over by buzzards searching and circling in their lazy, smudged circles, a fingerprint against the blue-and-white, sun-drenched sky, for something dead or dying. To the hunter's joy this is a home for the quick, small, apparitional wild turkey. And some of the oldest among the living will surely claim to have heard or even to have seen, in long-gone days, the last of the Florida panthers there; with, once in a while, a claimed hearing or sighting, even here or now, by some barely credible witness.

Oak trees don't really have beards or wigs, humans do. Another writer might have said, "Spanish moss grows on the trees" and left it at that. Insects don't orchestrate, that's a human activity. Technically, insects just buzz. Buzzards don't brood, their path in the sky is not a fingerprint. They are just big birds flying around in circles. Birdsong does not haunt a woods, the ghosts of humans do that. Just to show off, the author creates implied anthropomorphism with "apparitional wild turkey." Apparitions are ghosts, which conjure a human image; apparitional means ghostlike. He's telling us that wild turkeys hide in the brush, vanishing like ghosts. By investing these things with human characteristics he creates powerful images and a sense of magic.

You're sitting across a small round table from your favorite author in a cozy cafe in Paris. Ms. Author is prettier than her pictures, with long auburn hair and high cheekbones. She reminds you of Hilary Swank, the actress. A jazz trio plays softly in the next room. The bartender clinks glasses together as he washes them. You're sipping strong coffee and nibbling on a tray of seafood appetizers. An English gentleman strolls past puffing his pipe. The smoke isn't oppressive, it just perfumes the air. You cradle the warm coffee cup and smile. Your new friend has agreed to convey to you all the tricks that make her writing irresistible. This is your one chance to learn from your hero; you don't want to miss an instant.

Ms. Author brushes a strand of hair from her forehead and smiles, then reaches into her purse and pulls out a clothespin. "First," she says, "you must put this on your nose."

"Excuse me?" you say, confused.

"Clamp this on your nose."

You don't understand, but don't want to argue, so you clamp the clothespin on your nose. You feel self-conscious wearing a clothespin, but it seems a small price to pay. This is, after all, your favorite author. You would do whatever she asked.

"Excellent," she says. "Now this blindfold."

You had been enjoying watching her and noticing other customers walk by so you're disappointed at this new twist, but you comply. No wonder you hadn't been able to identify the tricks she employs. You never would have figured out the clothespin trick, let alone the blindfold. You start thinking about winning a Pulitzer.

"Put these on," she says, handing you a pair of heavy mittens. You do as instructed and can no longer feel the warmth and smoothness of your coffee cup.

"Now these earplugs. Wear them for five minutes, then remove them."

With the earplugs inserted firmly in your ears, wearing a blindfold, clothespin, and mittens, you no longer have any sense that you're in a cozy Parisian cafe. The jazz band disappears, there is no pipe tobacco smell. There's no point to sipping your coffee or nibbling on seafood because you can't taste them. Your mind begins to drift. You imagine you're in the middle of a Kansas cornfield, all alone and bored. There's no way to tell when five minutes have elapsed. You get drowsy and try not to doze. After you're sure that you've passed whatever sort of test this is, you remove the earplugs.

"That was fun," you lie. "What's next?

You hear the jazz band, and the bartender, and other customers, but your mentor says nothing.

"What's next?" you repeat in a more forceful voice, but she doesn't respond. You pull off the blindfold and realize she's gone. You remove the clothespin and gloves and see that she's written something on a napkin. It says, "Don't do that when you write."

Our senses inform us that we're alive and located somewhere. Without them, we may as well be in a coma or a math class. Each sense sends us information every instant and we process it without conscious effort. In some situations it's normal to focus on one sense: the scent of wood smoke leads us back to camp, the stop light changes to yellow and we accelerate, we bite into a habañero pepper and our eyes water.

As writers, it's easy to focus on one sense to the exclusion of the others. Our character sits in the sun and feels the heat on his face. Remarkably, he doesn't notice the smell of a newly mowed lawn or hear the airplane droning in the distance. He forgets the terrible taste in his mouth from trying to siphon gasoline two pages earlier. He doesn't notice the dew soaking his shirt or the pain from that bullet wound in his shoulder we inflicted on him in the last chapter.

Clearly, our character isn't the brightest bulb in the refrigerator: he notices only the sun on his face. If you were in the scene you'd see your surroundings, hear sounds, feel sensations, and smell the air. Without our senses, we don't feel immersed in the scene. We're watching television with the sound muted or listening to a video of a pretty young dancer with our eyes closed. It just doesn't seem natural.

You don't need to announce every airplane that buzzes above your character or let us smell each car's exhaust as it passes. Their inclusion or exclusion is a writer's choice. Each time you take advantage of a good opportunity to engage the reader's senses you enrich his experience. He feels more a part of the scene.

Here's a brief scene in *Travels with Charley* by John Steinbeck. As you read it, notice how he involves your senses:

> "...Come on, you might as well eat with us out back."
>
> Out back was kitchen, larder, pantry, dining room—and the cot covered with army blankets made it bedroom too. A great gothic wood stove clicked and purred. We were to eat at a square table covered with white, knife-scarred oilcloth. The keyed-up boy dished up bowls of bubbling navy beans and fat-back.

Steinbeck says what he has to say as efficiently as possible, then gets out of the way. He describes the setting effortlessly, the only way it could be described. If you look closer, you realize he's employed our visual sense (we see the cot covered with army blankets), and he's also added a sound track. The wood stove is clicking and purring, the beans are bubbling. If you know what beans and fat-back smell like, you also smell the scene and may be salivating to the phantom taste in your mouth. If not, imagine bacon sizzling. The knife-scarred oilcloth is visual, but somehow I find myself running my fingers over the cuts and feeling them as well. Of course, that's just me. It's probably an accident. You didn't notice yourself feeling the texture of that oilcloth did you?

For most of us, describing things visually feels natural. If we stretch, we might include some sounds. The sense of touch seems harder and beginning writers seldom engage our senses of smell or taste. That's a shame, because they can be powerful.

In *The Handmaid's Tale*, Margaret Atwood spends more than two pages describing a sitting room. She describes it in general terms, then describes it in a sort of literary analogy:

> "The sitting room is subdued, symmetrical; it's one of the shapes money takes when it freezes. Money has

trickled through this room for years and years, as if through an underground cavern, crusting and hardening like stalactites into these forms."

Then she uses the sense of sight, including "the dusk-rose velvet of the drawn drapes ... the cow's tongue hush of the tufted Chinese rug on the floor with its pink peonies, the suave leather of the Commander's chair, the glint of brass on the box beside it." Then she devotes an entire paragraph to the way the room smells:

> The room smells of lemon oil, heavy cloth, fading daffodils, the leftover smells of cooking that have made their way from the kitchen or the dining room, and of Serena Joy's perfume: Lily of the Valley. Perfume is a luxury, she must have some private source. I breathe it in, thinking I should appreciate it. It's the scent of prepubescent girls, of the gifts young children used to give their mothers, for Mother's Day; the smell of white cotton socks and white flesh not yet given over to hairiness and blood. It makes me feel slightly ill, as if I'm in a closed car on a hot muggy day with an older woman wearing too much face powder. This is what the sitting room is like, despite its elegance.
>
> I would like to steal something from this room.

If you are a fan of Margaret Atwood, by now you share her desire to steal something from the room: you want to steal her trick of describing things in terms of many senses.

Gabriel Garcia Marquez employs the senses in a way that feels much different but just as effective in the opening lines of *Love in the Time of Cholera*:

> It was inevitable: the scent of bitter almonds always reminded him of the fate of unrequited love. Dr. Juvenal Urbino noticed it as soon as he entered the still darkened house where he had hurried on an urgent call to attend a case that for him had lost all urgency many years before. The Antillean refugee Jeremiah de Saint-

Armour, disabled war veteran, photographer of children, and his most sympathetic opponent in chess, had escaped the torments of memory with the aromatic fumes of gold cyanide.

The sense of smell dominates this passage, but we also see the darkened house and perhaps a vague image of photographs of children. Another example, this one from *The English Patient* by Michael Ondaatje:

The man named Caravaggio pushes open all the windows in the room so he can hear the noises of the night. He undresses, rubs his palms gently over his neck and for a while lies down on the unmade bed. The noise of the trees, the breaking of moon into silver fish bouncing off the leaves of asters outside.

The moon is on him like skin, a sheaf of water. An hour later he is on the roof of the villa. Up on the peak he is aware of the shelled sections along the slope of roofs, the two acres of destroyed gardens and orchards that neighbour the villa. He looks over where they are in Italy.

Certainly we *see* some things in this scene, but we are also asked to bring other senses into the scene in a neat oblique way. When he rubs his palms over his neck, we *feel* the tactile sensation even though he doesn't specifically say what it feels like. We all know. He mentions noises of the night, specifically the trees. We feel the moonlight on him, sort of, and it feels like a warm, wet sheet to me. Describing the moonlight on the moving leaves as the breaking of moon into silver fish seems exquisitely cool to me. I've never seen that before, yet it created an instant visual image in my brain. You might also notice that the guy does not always write in complete sentences and loves passive verbs. An English teacher might deduct points, but winning the Booker Prize and selling the movie rights probably eases that sting.

Clichés

Shakespeare shot analogies into our language the way an automatic rifle shoots bullets into a bale of straw. He coined phrases like "coining phrases" and a thousand others that worked so well we adopted them.

Whenever someone invents a good phrase, people repeat it. And repeat it, and repeat it. Before long, its original zest dissipates. No one remembers how creative it sounded 400 years ago; they don't remember Shakespeare or anyone else as its author. They certainly don't remember the latest parrot that squawked it out.

A joke isn't as funny the second time you hear it. It has even less effect the fiftieth time. Similarly, every phrase dims a bit each time it's used.

Expressions that have been drained of all color by repetition are called clichés. Let me be clear here: Clichés are evil, wasteful, stupid and condescending. Do not use them.

Clichés bore your reader the way a television commercial does when it's rerun too many times. They don't feel original or interesting, because they're not. They waste space; they occupy territory you could have filled with original words. Someone who wants to read Shakespeare doesn't need you. Clichés suggest the writer doesn't possess original thoughts, or is criminally lazy, or thinks the reader too dull to notice. Clichés make writers sound stupid.

Unfortunately, the little pests are seductive. While we're scratching out a first draft, clichés often seem like the one inescapably correct way to express an idea. When we "coin a phrase" or "leap to a conclusion" or "sink like a stone" we feel like fine, original writers. Actually we're just typing phrases Shakespeare or Ben Franklin or someone else created. Many things sink like stones – why not freshen your writing by creating your own image? "He sank like an anchor" conveys the same lack of buoyancy. Depending on the precise flavor you're trying to cook up, your choices are limitless. Maybe he sank like a refrigerator, or a broken hard-drive, or an old army boot, or a rifle. Why cheat yourself of the fun of making things sink weirdly?

People use clichés for three reasons. First, sometimes they don't recognize them. They may have not read enough to feel flogged by a phrase. Therefore, they think it's cool and no one will notice or care that it's been used before.

Second, they may not realize the coma-inducing effect of clichés. Familiar phrases feel comfortable, as if they'd been validated and approved by some authority. "Hard as a rock" seems synonymous with "very hard." It sounds just fine. Everyone will understand, so what's the harm? If someone else used the image, why can't I? Because I say so, that's why.

But the big reason writers lean on these ancient crutches is laziness. Shoot, the guy did sink like a stone, didn't he? Readers will understand, it's more effective than "he sank quickly," and I've got more sentences to write today. Anyway, everyone uses clichés, right? Right. Everyone except the writers you admire. If you watch carefully, you'll see that they capture wild, untamed phrases and train them for the meek to ride. Do you want to fill your pages with sleek stallions or petting-zoo ponies?

You can't quit clichés cold turkey. Oops. I meant to say, you've been driving the cliché truck so long your head will crash into the windshield if you suddenly slam on the brakes. Just be aware of them and avoid the ones you notice. The more clichés you use, the more amateurish and ordinary your writing will seem. If you notice yourself writing a familiar sentence or phrase, experiment with more original alternatives. Your readers paid for your words, no one else's.

Scenes, ideas, and characters can become cliché. In silent movies, so many villains tied heroines to railroad tracks the cliché inspired humorous popular songs. This horrifying image became a joke. The story of Adam and Eve has been retold in so many variations it's lost all power. So many heroes have been locked in seemingly inescapable situations only to have the bad guy leave and the hero escape that it inspired a comic bit in Austin Powers. The cavalry rescued so many western heroes that not only did the scene become a cliché, so did the phrase "send in the cavalry." If the idea is so familiar it's been satirized, it's a cliché. If you've read it before, it's probably a cliché. If you've read it before, you didn't really create it, did you? You stole it.

If your scenes sink (like stones) to such familiar depths, you'll have to send in the cavalry to rescue them. Or throw them out with the bath water.

Hip Words, Daddio, Are the Bees' Knees

Every generation adopts certain words, uses them to death, and then forgets to bury them. For a time in the late 20th century, everything was "awesome." This glorious ten-dollar word once meant something that inspired awe, the way meeting God would. With repetition, its value declined until it described a pleasant CD or well-cooked hamburger. Finally, the word became so cheap a starving man wouldn't make the effort to pick one up from the sidewalk. No one wanted a CD that was merely "awesome," because everything was awesome. They didn't even want one that was "totally awesome."

Beware of popular words and phrases. Their familiarity quickly spoils them and dates your immortal prose.

Modifiers and the Modifiers that Modify Them

To "modify" something means to change it. In language, modifiers are words designed to add to the meaning of other words.

Adjectives modify nouns. In the phrase "the big dog," big is the adjective. It changes the meaning of the word dog. Nothing wrong with a fine adjective, but often a more precise noun eliminates the need for one.

Adverbs augment verbs. Whenever you feel tempted to add an adverb, evaluate the verb you started with. If "he ran" doesn't convey your image, and you think "he ran fast" comes closer, take a look at the verb "ran." Maybe he galloped, or raced, or sprinted. The best adverb in the world is still one more word you're forcing onto your tired reader. It's an extra coal car that won't help pull your train.

71

Your choice of modifiers reflects your personality. Until this book, I've never used the word "utterly," while Annie Dillard has never written a book without it. Besides her fame, success, admiring fans, and Pulitzer Prize, this is the easiest way to distinguish our "voices."

A modifier can modify another modifier, and you can keep that chain going forever; "the big dog" could become "the remarkably big dog." *Remarkably* modifies the word *big*, which we already agreed was a modifier. If you wanted, it could transform into the "the unusually remarkable big dog." Why not just start with the largest St. Bernard in the world and forget trying to patch up the image with modifiers?

Ideally, modifiers improve the word they modify, but overused modifiers don't do a thing except take up space on the page. For example, "very" and "really" no longer mean anything. What's the difference between a big elephant and a very big elephant? In the reader's mind there's no difference at all. The tiny effort you forced him to expend reading "very" yielded no reward. Even if he expended a very tiny effort, he'll hate you a little for it. Or, if it makes you feel better, he'll hate you a very little.

When you notice yourself trying to inflate a word by inserting "very" or "really," you probably started with an undersized word. That elephant wasn't *very big*, it was huge, or immense, or gargantuan, or colossal. Colossal is like really, really, really big. Saying it was very colossal won't make it grow. We can't tell the difference between a CD that's awesome, one that's totally awesome, and one that's very totally awesome. But we know an excellent CD when we hear one.

Choose modifiers carefully. If they don't pull their weight, don't hitch them up. Using modifiers to improve other modifiers is like painting a barn, then trying to improve the color by painting a different shade on top of the first one. Better to start with the right color.

This principal also works in reverse, when you want to diminish another word slightly. If you write "the man was sad," then decide that conveys a deeper depression than you intended, don't change to "The man was a little sad." Write sentences that are more vivid than reality; diminishing them is counterproductive. We're already reading your words through a number of reducing lenses. When we read "the man was sad," we don't assume he was ready to kill himself, just that he was having a bad morning. If he's described as a "little sad" we assume he was only the tiniest bit sad and will probably be fine in a few minutes. On the other hand, maybe he was abject, or morose, maybe even suicidal. Can he feel a little suicidal? Would you rather be a little bit elated or pretty happy? I'd rather be joyful, or ecstatic; your readers would, too.

You can inadvertently dim your own lovely words by repeating them. If everyone in your story is "ecstatic," they will all seem merely happy. Not even really happy. If all your characters are huge, none will seem especially large. By the time events snowball out of control three or four times, all your snow will have melted, soaking any other clichés you have imposed on the reader.

That's not to say, as Ben Franklin would, that modifiers should be thrown out with the bath water, as some insist. The writers I admire use them judiciously. If your favorite authors do as well, let them be your guide. Notice words as you read. Modifiers can make fine jewelry for your sentences, but don't let your manuscript leave the house dressed like a tramp. Select bold and original modifiers with the same care as verbs. Don't weigh your sentences down with cheap, clumsy, overworked modifiers.

And don't listen to me. Open your favorite book to a scene you like and notice how the author uses modifiers. If her character is a little sad while he's running very fast, and you feel tears sort of welling up in your eyes, then ignore me somewhat and kind of steer your writing by that star. But if her dejected hero races toward the subway, and you're entranced, note the technique. The point is this: read your favorite author carefully, noticing how she handles these issues, just like you read my previous two sentences. The only "right" way is the one you like. It takes practice to read like a writer but it's great fun.

We only have three choices of "tense." We can write in the past, the present, or the future. "He *is* happy" is present tense, "he *was* happy" is past tense, "he *will be* happy" is future tense. You can write in any that you like, but be consistent. When wrapped up in our imaginary worlds we writers can forget who we are; sometimes we even forget *when* we are. If we forget, our readers will too. Most books are written in past tense, as if a storyteller was relating something that has already happened. Terry McMillan wrote *How Stella Got her Groove Back* in present tense, and this is how it sounds:

> I feel bad. Maybe I was too hard on Judas is what I'm thinking after I wake up this morning and get ready to put on my jogging clothes then change my mind fast. I'm tired of running on the beach. This is my last day here. I have run on that beach every single morning I've been here and besides I do not want to run into him this morning. In fact I don't want to see Mr. Freak of the Week for the duration of my stay if it's at all possible.

She makes it sound like we're right beside her while she talks. She's telling us her current thoughts, not writing a report of last week's events.

Readers notice when we change tense. If we've been writing in the past tense: "he was in the barn," or "it was raining," it jolts them when we shift into the present or future tense, even if it's grammatically sound and reasonable to do so. Maybe the barn still exists, so we might say, "He was in the barn, which is red." But if we do that, especially in a more complex example, our reader will re-read the sentence to make sure she didn't miss something. Better to say "He was in the red barn" which eliminates the problem. If you can't do that, try to keep your tenses consistent. He was in the barn which was red. Maybe the barn is still red, but who cares? We don't want to stop our reader. We didn't want to yesterday when we wrote it, we don't want to today which was in the past from your perspective, and we won't want to when you are reading this, right now, here, in the future from my perspective when I was writing this.

And yet every writer does this sometimes; we get caught up in what we're writing and don't notice. Imagine that you're writing this scene:

> Jim crept up the creepy old staircase. He moved slowly, listening to each step creak. Lightning struck outside, he froze in his tracks, but knew he could not stop. He had to reach that door at the top of the stairs...

As the writer you probably know what's going to jump out at him when he opens that door but it still makes you nervous. You lean into your keyboard and keep writing.

> He stopped at top of the stairs. He reaches for the door handle. Slowly he turns it. He pushes open the door...

Oops. We slipped from past tense into present tense and many of our readers went back down the stairs and out the door. It's just that easy for it to happen, and if you talk in the present tense a lot ("So I'm going down the street, minding my own business, see, and this guy steps in front of me and wants to talk ...") it won't bother you. But most readers will feel the cosmic shift in their imaginary world's orbit and feel unbalanced. If it doesn't bother you, be especially careful, because you'll do it without noticing. You don't want your writing to be accidental and automatic. If you decide to fluctuate between tenses, fine, that's your choice. But if the books you love don't, or you don't know whether they do or not, consider what that means. Why do you think another reader will like something you don't like yourself?

Unnecessary words clutter your writing and cost the reader effort without a compensating reward. Eliminate clutter.

After you've trimmed unnecessary modifiers, search for redundancy. "The nocturnal bird sang only at night" repeats information. Nocturnal birds conduct all their business, including singing, at night. If you say "he woke up at 9 a.m. in the morning" you've done the same thing. Nine a.m. only happens in the morning.

Extra words love to creep into introductory phrases. If you say, "In my humble opinion, according to the best data available to me, the government needs to pass this law," you're spending most of your time on stage clearing your throat. We know it's your opinion. We assume you base that opinion on the information you have. When you eliminate the throat clearing, you're left with, "The government needs to pass this law," which is what you wanted to say. The reader focuses on your message rather than your stage fright.

Some writers have moments of such brilliance we forgive them their messes. Extremely fast readers don't seem bothered by navigating around piles of extra words. If you love Dickens (who got paid by the word), for example, or Proust, you may be this kind of reader, and you should feel free to emulate their luxurious long sentences without feeling any guilt for filling extended single thoughts full to the brim just because they require a more focused sort of concentration from the reader than our current short-attention-spanned society usually demands or even tolerates. If your favorite author averages fifteen words per sentence, however, and yours average forty-three, you might consider trimming fat.

Throw Mama From the Train a Kiss:
Structural Ambiguity and Pronouns

Inside the dumpster, he found a hat. It was painted red.

The word "it" could refer either to the dumpster or the hat, but because of its proximity to "hat," the reader assumes you mean there's a red hat inside the dumpster. If you intended to throw a black hat into a red dumpster, you missed. Pronouns like "it" or "he" refer to someone or something mentioned earlier, usually the last thing mentioned. If you're careless, you'll sprinkle your work with unintended humor. Even if one can deduce your intent by the context, readers make the assumption conveyed by the sentence structure first and, if you're lucky, revise their understanding later. Structural ambiguity slows them down and irritates.

John shot the robber. He got up and did a little dance. He bled to death on the floor.

After we think about it, we know what you probably meant, but you've created several different possible meanings by being careless with your pronouns. The "he" doing the dance might be the unfortunate robber and John might be bleeding to death. Or John might be dancing before he bleeds to death. If we must finish the paragraph before we can interpret its sentences, the syntax (the order of the words) has created ambiguity.

You can eliminate it (the ambiguity) simply by noticing it and rewriting. "John shot the robber, then did a little dance. The robber bled to death on the floor."

Words like "only" can also confuse if you don't place them near the words they describe. "I only bought milk because I knew you were coming over," probably means that the only reason I bought milk was because I expected you. I don't drink it myself. But perhaps I would have bought some bottled water in addition to the milk if I'd realized you were bringing a date. In that case you mean "I bought only milk." Keep "only" close to the word or phrase it limits.

The word "since" creates a weird kind of ambiguity when used to mean "because." Its precise meaning relates to time: "I've been sad since you left me." If you use it instead of "because," readers will assume you're referring to time.

"Since the Civil War divided America, Martin Luther King carefully avoided inflammatory language." Martin Luther King may well have been careful, but he didn't start being careful in 1865. He wasn't careful for a hundred years. What I meant to say was that he chose his words carefully because of the divisiveness of the Civil War. On the other hand, I might say, "Since the Civil War, civil rights have progressed dramatically." This is fine because I'm referring to time. Notice I didn't say, "This is fine since I'm referring to time."

Or Not

There's a danger to all this talk about adding vivid verbs, great analogies, sensory images, and important details. The danger is that you'll actually take my advice.

Most people will never use vivid verbs and metaphor, despite their effectiveness, no matter how I rant. On the other hand, a few people will see these tips, not as a way to spice their writing, but as a whole new diet. It will become a religion to them. From now on, they vow, every description will be bold and metaphoric, every verb will launch itself off the page and into the reader's face, every paragraph will smell like something, sound like something, and taste like something.

For those few people: relax. Elegance is usually simple and direct. Sometimes you just have to tell us the guy is tall, thin, and wearing a brown shirt. That this guy climbs into his red Jeep and takes a three-by-five card out of his shirt pocket. That he reads it and frowns, then shrugs and starts the engine. No metaphors, no powerful verbs, no blinding reflections or overpowering stenches. We need to get that Jeep started and the smartest way to do that is to turn the darn key. If we invest too much of our newfound literary magic in the starting of the jeep, the incident itself will become noteworthy, and superstitious readers will thereafter avoid Jeeps altogether.

Don't spout brilliant nonesense. Use your powers selectively and only for good and worthy purposes.

The Overall Flow of any Work

Curiosity

I dislike reviews that reveal too much, especially those that tell me how a book or movie ends. They douse the fun of a writer engaging my curiosity. Worse is a writer who douses it himself. Curiosity pulls a reader through any book, article, or essay. An article draws us in with the promise of interesting information. A novel entices us with the promise of learning about the characters and discovering how the story ends. Good writers make us curious about a hundred details along the way. What will this minor character do? How will that one react? Will the meteor hit the earth? Will the fair maiden dump the jerk? Will he retaliate?

One way to create curiosity is to drop clues along the way. These may be overt, like the maiden threatening to drop the jerk if he gets drunk one more time. Or clues may be subtle: the maiden buys a plane ticket and doesn't tell the jerk. Now the reader has information that carries an unstated question: why did she buy the plane ticket? Is it for him, or her, or her mother? Is she going to leave him? We turn the pages, eager to discover the answer.

The masters of creating curiosity write with a special confidence. They know answers to dozens of questions a reader might have, but they don't blurt them all out at once. The maiden removes a plane ticket from its hiding place, fondles it for a moment, smiles, and then hides it again.

"Wait a minute!" the reader screams. "Where did she get that plane ticket? Why is she keeping it hidden?" But the writer ignores these questions and moves on. "All in good time," he seems to say.

Sometimes curiosity arises from the language itself rather than the meaning. Here's the first paragraph from *Adventures of Huckleberry Finn* by Mark Twain, a book that's been selling well for over 100 years:

> You don't know about me without you have read a book by the name of *The Adventures of Tom Sawyer*, but that ain't no matter. That book was made by Mr. Mark

Twain and he told the truth, mainly. There was things which he stretched, but mainly he told the truth. That is nothing. I never seen anybody but lied one time or another, without it was Aunt Polly or the widow, or maybe Mary. Aunt Polly – Tom's Aunt Polly she is – and Mary and the Widow Douglas is all told about in that book, which is mostly a true book, with some stretchers as I said before.

Does this paragraph make you ask, "Who in the world is this uneducated speaker and why did somebody publish his book?" Do you smile as you realize that Huck the character has come to life so vigorously he's making fun of the writer who wrote him and, in fact, calls him a liar? Do you feel the urge to keep reading? If so, it's no accident. Mark Twain could craft sentences masterfully when it suited him, or when someone irritated him. By poking fun at himself and all writers and readers he buys our interest, makes us curious, and another generation purchases his book.

We trust the writer to answer our questions sooner or later. If he fails to, we will despise him. Good writers create many questions, some to answer within a few sentences, others to remain mysteries until we've done our part and read the book. Each answered question increases our confidence in him.

Beginning writers think they need to provide overwhelming detail early so the book feels realistic. But readers don't demand all the information at once if they trust the writer. When the bank robber curses his wooden leg, we want to know how he lost the limb, but not before he escapes the bank. We trust the writer to fill us in when he's ready.

Wise writers begin a work by creating a strong curiosity to propel the reader through the difficult terrain of setting up the story. As they lay this groundwork, they sprinkle in additional sources of curiosity, each one tugging the reader along. If they fail to create sufficient curiosity, the reader will soon become bored no matter how eloquent the sentences. Years ago, readers had longer attention spans, fewer distractions, and a stronger confidence in writers. They tolerated many pages of background information before tossing the book aside. Today's readers are less generous and will give you about a page to hook them. At big publishing companies, editors often reject manuscripts after a few paragraphs.

Here's the first sentence of *Sunset Limited* by James Lee Burke. Does it make you curious to continue reading, or discourage you by its graphic nature?

> I had seen a dawn like this one only twice in my life: once in Vietnam, after a Bouncing Betty had risen from the earth on a night trail and twisted its tentacles of light around my thighs, and years earlier outside of Franklin, Louisiana, when my father and I discovered the body of a labor organizer who had been crucified with sixteen-penny nails, ankle and wrist, against a barn wall.

I admire Clive Cussler's ability to create curiosity. Many nights I've started one of his books and been unable to put it down. After losing too much sleep, I think I've figured out his secret. He starts chapters with a huge event, an insurmountable problem, something no reasonable reader could ignore. Over the course of the chapter that problem is dealt with. Then, as the chapter ends, he springs a new problem on me. I say, "Okay, I'll just read the first page of the next chapter." But on the next page the world is disintegrating beneath our hero's feet and I can't abandon him. I describe it this way: He starts every chapter with an explosion and ends every chapter with a lit fuse.

This isn't a rule; it's my own observation. A different author may keep you up at night with another strategy. Look at her writing from a dispassionate perch and figure out how she does it to you. As examples, I could have picked the ending of virtually any chapter in any of Cussler's books. Using *Raise the Titanic*, I created a list of about twenty, and was getting sucked into his story so had to stop. I'll give you a couple at random.

He ends one chapter this way:

> Who were the eight men he claimed to have murdered?
>
> What was the secret of the vault?
>
> They were questions that were to haunt Bigalow for the next seventy-six years, right up to the last few hours of his life

And another chapter this way:

> "And where are you going to find this paragon of virtue?"
>
> "I'm awfully glad you used the word virtue," Sandecker said slyly. "You see, I was thinking of your wife."

Clive tends to start the next chapter with a different scene, or a different character, or a different problem. He strings us along in this new mode while we remain curious about what happened at the end of the previous chapter. He does this to us over and over again. Sure, Clive writes suspense books and his job description is creating curiosity. But curiosity pulls us through every book, essay, article, and short story.

Here is how David Guterson opens his book *Snow Falling on Cedars*, a book considered more literary than suspense:

> The accused man, Kabuo Miyamoto, sat proudly upright with a rigid grace, his palms placed softly on the defendant's table—the posture of a man who has detached himself insofar as this is possible at his own trial.

Does that make you curious enough to read one more sentence? No huge fireworks, but a quiet sort of questioning. We feel drawn into the scene because we can see Kabuo sitting there and wonder why he's calm, why he's proud, why he has a rigid grace, and why he's on trial. The first sentence of the book creates at least four unstated questions.

Mary Stuart ends chapters with a big question, then starts the next chapter, not by answering it, but by leaving us hanging while she asks another question. Here is the end of one chapter in her book *The Hollow Hills:*

> As the sword left his grip it fell, through his hands and through mine, and between us to the ground. I knelt, groping in the darkness, but my hand met nothing. I could feel his breath above me, warm as a living man's, and his cloak brushed my cheek. I heard him say: "Find it. There is no one else who can find it." Then my eyes were open and it was full noon, and the strawberry mare was nuzzling at me where I lay, with her mane brushing my face.

As I turn to the next chapter I have several questions. If he was not a living man, what was he? Who found the sword? Why is the main character the only one who can find it? Was this a dream? What happened to all that time, did the main character just sleep until noon? Gullible child that I am, I turn to the next chapter, eager for answers, and this is what I read:

> December is certainly no time for traveling, especially for one whose business does not allow him to use the roads.

Great. Now, besides all our questions about the sword/dream scene, we wonder who's traveling and what their business is that makes them take the back roads. We've got no choice. We've got to keep reading.

Tension and suspense are variations on curiosity, with one little twist: when we expect something bad to happen to our character, we get tense and feel suspense. To create tension, give us reason to believe something bad is going to happen. At least make us believe something interesting is going to happen. Uncertainty of any kind creates a kind of tension.

Journalists try to create curiosity by beginning newspaper articles with stories: "Little Jimmy Smith sits among toys he'll never get to play with again." They go on to describe the trailer Jimmy lives in, his poor but honest parents, and his medical condition. Three paragraphs later we learn that the story is really about some new gene therapy and the company that just patented it.

That may work for some readers but it annoys me. I wasted time becoming curious about a character who wasn't the subject of the story. Whenever I see poor Jimmy in the first line of an article, I skip down to where the information begins. If the information doesn't interest me, and the writer fails to spark my curiosity, I don't read the article. Poor Jimmy has fooled me too many times and I'm wise to him.

Which is to say, don't insult your reader by trying to create phony curiosity. If the airplane ticket has no significance, leave it hidden in the drawer.

On the other hand, if curiosity about the ticket is intentional misdirection (perhaps in a mystery) it's worth the risk. If you wave your right hand around wildly we expect sparks to fly from it sooner or later. If they don't, but you pull a rabbit out of a hat with your left hand, we'll forgive you. Otherwise, you're just waving bye-bye to your readers.

Sometimes I throw in a question that occurs to me, even though I don't know the answer myself, in hopes it will answer itself as I write. Curiosity can pull a *writer* through a project, too. No reason to let readers have all the fun.

Choosing Details

A good detective notices the most important details of a scene and so does a good writer. Clumsy detectives notice random details and report them all in their little notebooks, but not you. You are Sherlock Holmes and always asking, "What is important?" Details define both the scene and the writer who chose them.

Perhaps we step with you into a teenage boy's bedroom. We can't fully describe the overwhelming clutter before our reader drifts off to sleep. We have to choose. Do we smell incense that may mask some other variety of smoke? Are the walls covered with pictures of fast cars, rock groups, or pretty women? Do we see books on making bombs or no books at all? Are CDs strewn carelessly or neatly stored in alphabetical order? Are all the shirts black? Is a diary obvious on the bed, or do we find charred remains of a diary in a waste can?

You might choose certain details if the boy just discovered a cure for cancer in his biology lab, and others if he committed suicide. A detective looks for different clues based on the situation, and so will your reader.

Readers are smart. If you choose your details wisely, they'll understand your point. You won't have to explain it and they'll resent it if you do. Look around the room again. Every book in the room is in alphabetical order, and so are the CDs, and even the posters. This kid loves organization. So isn't it odd that the "C" portion of the music collection is with the "R's?" You don't need to expound, just report it. I'm curious – I'm already trying to explain it myself. Aren't you? Later, when we're trying to find the CD-ROM from the boy's computer containing his cancer data, your reader will be way ahead of the narrator. The boy hid it with his music CDs among the "C's" for "cancer." Someone broke into his room and stole it, but when they replaced the CDs they were careless. They didn't put them back in the correct order. Your reader will love the sense that he's smarter than the author. He'll also be curious to learn if he's right and eager to see when the author catches up to him.

John Berendt, who wrote *Midnight in the Garden of Good and Evil*, is a master of choosing details. Here he spends exactly one paragraph describing a character by choosing which details of the man's life to share with us:

> Bubsy Ryan was a good ol' boy. He liked to go fishing, hunting, and drinking. He had a full head of touseled brown hair, long reddish sideburns, and bags under his eyes that made him look permanently hung over. He got along well with the police; he was good at horse-trading and had a folksy, drawling courtroom manner. Bubsy argued every major murder case himself, but it was no secret that his management of the prosecutor's

office was casual at best, just as it had been under his father. A backlog of over a thousand untried cases stretched back twenty-five years. Bubsy enjoyed being D.A., but he admitted it did have its drawbacks. "You're limited in some ways," he said. "You can't go out drinkin' with your wife, 'cause you'll read about it in the paper the next day."

Stephen King chooses details in a cunning way to create a much different effect. He fills his books with tidbits remarkable only for their ordinariness. People drink the same brands of soft drink I drink, they drive cars I've owned, they watch my favorite television shows. His goal is to convince us that his stories occur in the ordinary world, that they really could happen. We believe each detail because we've watched that show while drinking that drink. We slip easily into his world because it's our own world. As we read, we're sitting on our couch, just like his character is, sipping Diet Pepsi along with him, watching *Wheel of Fortune*, using the remote to flip to a *Star Trek* rerun, thinking that this book isn't scary at all. It's just like our own life. The single element that hasn't happened to us is the girl ringing our doorbell who sets things on fire with her mind. By the time we notice smoke rising from our Nikes, it's too late to douse the fire with our Pepsi. We believed everything else, so we believe this too.
Here's how King starts *The Dark Half*:

The May 23 issue of People magazine was pretty typical.

The cover was graced by that week's Dead Celebrity, a rock and roll star who had hanged himself in a jail cell after being taken into custody for possession of cocaine and assorted satellite drugs. Inside was the usual smorgasbord: nine unsolved sex murders in the desolate western half of Nebraska; a health-food guru who had been busted for kiddie porn; a Maryland housewife who had grown a squash that looked a bit like a bust of Jesus Christ—if you looked at it with your eyes half-closed in a dim room, that was; a game paraplegic girl training for the Big Apple Bike-A-Thon; a Hollywood divorce; a New York society marriage; a wrestler recovering from a heart attack; a comedian fighting a palimony suit.

In one paragraph he's got me believing that his characters live in the same world I live in. Shoot, I think I read that issue of People magazine.

In *Newjack*, Ted Conover becomes a prison guard at Sing Sing for the purpose of writing about the experience. His language is never flashy, he simply reports what goes on. The details he chooses to report give us all our information. To describe the gym, he spends little time on physical description or measurements. He just puts himself in the scene and tells us what he sees:

> Beyond these activities, the gym held many surprises. On a busy day, it seemed almost like a bazaar. A dozen fans of Days of Our Lives gathered religiously every day for the latest installment of their favorite soap. Behind them, regular games of Scrabble, chess, checkers, and bridge were conducted with great seriousness. (One of the bridge players, known as Drywall—a white-bearded man with dreadlocks—came from 5-Building; more than once when he was late, his partners asked me to call the officers over there and make sure he'd left so they could start their game.) At the table next to the games, an older man sold hand-painted greeting cards for all occasions to raise money for the Jaycees, one of Sing Sing's "approved inmate organizations." In a far corner behind the weight area, at the bottom of a small flight of stairs, a regular group of inmates practiced some kind of martial art. Martial arts were forbidden by the rules, but these guys were so pointedly low-key, and the rule seemed to me so ill conceived, that I didn't break it up. In the men's bathroom, inmates smoked—also against the rules but, from what I could tell, tacitly accepted.

The main character of *Newjack* or any of Ted's books is himself, the narrator. Ted the author develops Ted the character with every word he writes. As we look around that prison gym with him, he demonstrates by the details he chooses that inmates fascinate him. A different author might have focused on the building, or its history, or the laws that had been broken to put everyone in that gym. So, while we learn a lot about Sing Sing, and the prisoners, and the system, over the course of the book we get the reward we're usually looking for: we get to live someone's life with them. While we're reading, we're fascinated by inmates, just like Ted the main character. Our experience of being a guard in Sing Sing is controlled by the details Ted the author chooses to relate to us.

Authenticity

You've probably heard the cliché "write what you know." The truth in the saying has been lost by unthinking repetition. A strict constructionist would prohibit you from writing science fiction or any other imaginative work. You can't possibly know what Mars is really like, therefore you can't set your story there. That's not the useful message of "write what you know." It isn't a prohibition, but an invitation.

Use your own experiences to make your words feel authentic. If you've worked for a magazine all your life, your wealth of knowledge about that industry might fascinate me. Press releases, advertising deadlines, and color separations seem deadly dull and commonplace to you – why would anyone write about them? Because, to most of us, they are as exotic and unfamiliar as the rituals of the Pope's bodyguards. But even if your story allows no room for details of the magazine industry, you've dealt with advertising salesmen, stingy employers, and disorganized artists. A guy selling full-page color ads isn't much different than a guy selling shovels to miners in the old West or a guy selling trinkets and tribbles to space travelers. Taking advantage of your experiences lends authenticity to your writing.

"Write what you know" also reminds you to be careful when describing things you've never done and places you've never been. If you've never been to Denver and you place your story there, you're taking a huge risk. The first time you put mountains east of town, you'll lose all your Colorado readers. When you add a magnolia tree, you'll get angry mail. If you're a carpenter, your reader will enjoy the little touches of expertise you slip in. If you're not, your character may screw things together that ought to be nailed and glue things that anyone else would bolt. None of it will ring true. Don't try to fool the reader.

But you needn't confine yourself to your own life. Write any life you like, just do whatever homework is necessary.

Rather than "write what you know" I like "write what interests you." If you're genuinely interested, I will be too. Oddly enough, for the duration of the story, readers become interested in virtually anything. If you're fascinated by a particular kind of scorpion, and have studied it and kept one as a pet, readers will be drawn with you into that strange fascination. But if you're not particularly interested in something, even if you think you should be, we'll be bored right along with you. The murder of the President's daughter ought to be compelling, you think, so you assume your audience will eagerly follow your twisting plot. An asteroid ending all life on Earth ought to get anyone's attention. But, if the author isn't genuinely intrigued himself, we just won't care. Readers are never more interested in anything than the author is.

If you're human, when you write emotions, you are writing what you know. You've experienced all the emotions of your characters. You've felt angry, embarrassed, depressed, and exuberant. If your character is angry, remember your own anger and describe that. If your character's dog dies, describe how it felt when you lost someone you loved. Don't try to put yourself in the character's position and imagine. Put the character in your position and remember.

Themes and Plots

All writers love certain ideas that influence their writing.

These idea or "themes" become underlying "messages," usually hidden so that most readers notice them only on a subconscious level. In the movie *Napoleon Dynamite* each character gives something that is valuable to the receiver and acquires a kind of quiet dignity as a result. Most people who watch the movie will never notice that, yet some will sense the transformative power of giving. They just won't know where it came from.

When Steinbeck wrote *The Grapes of Wrath*, he must have been interested in human dignity, the redeeming value of optimism, and people helping each other. Was he consciously trying to animate these ideas? Not necessarily, but maybe. Themes inform a work whether or not the author expresses them specifically.

Plot is the unfolding of a story, the sequence of events, the overcoming of obstacles, the decisions characters make. Plot is what happens in a book or story. Writers often fuss over their plots, but they rarely fuss over their themes. They may map out a story line before writing the first word and decide what should happen in a book based on what would create a compelling story. Nothing wrong with that.

Shakespeare, on the other hand, rarely wrote an original plot. Like many others, he used existing stories or historical events as his plots. He just flat stole them. Unlike lesser writers, he imposed themes onto these stories. In *Romeo and Juliet* we watch two kids fall in love and try to make it work despite the obstacles of their circumstances. That premise isn't special; it plays nightly on television comedies. Shakespeare brought to life a larger idea: the power of love as it struggles against prejudice. This underlying theme elevates his play above the plot. The TV show *Will and Grace* also contains characters who love each other despite obstacles and prejudice, but in this case it creates humor. Ann Rice writes enchanting books in which vampires struggle against each other and against humans. Many horrible books have similar plots; hers rise above the genre because she explores man's yearning for power and immortality, and the price this yearning exacts.

Most fine writing involves larger ideas. Theme-free writing may entertain, but it feels superficial.

Ideas that intrigue you will find their way onto the page whether you want them to or not. Perhaps you want to write a book about cowboy bank robbers. No need to consider larger themes, right? Of course not. But there's a reason that's the book you want to write, even if you don't consciously know what it is. Maybe Robin Hood characters and their social impulses fascinate you. Maybe you find the idea of seeking a moral high ground by breaking laws a romantic one. Or maybe bank robbers are evil incarnate for you because they put their own desires above the good of their communities. If you're lucky enough to identify the reason you're drawn to a story, you'll find additional satisfaction in writing it.

But don't be too obvious. If you simply state your idea, perhaps "the world would be better if people were kinder to each other," you'll lose all the impact. Don't tell the reader your theme, let them come to it themselves. No one likes to be lectured to or preached at. Ideally, a reader will sense something larger beyond your words but be unable to express it precisely. Plant your idea so deeply in their mind they can't focus on it or argue with it but will continue to think about the book and its mysterious power long after they've forgotten the details of the story.

Good TV shows employ themes as well, and they're an easy place to begin studying them. Successful shows that received critical acclaim almost certainly have underlying themes in each episode. You can't watch old episodes of *Star Trek, Friends, Taxi, Frasier, Seinfeld, The Simpsons* or *The West Wing* without noticing themes. Those shows did not simply hatch fully formed; someone wrote them and used the tricks you're trying to learn.

Once you focus on themes, you may discover that plot dilemmas disappear from your path. Do the bank robbers ride off into the sunset or do they gallop off a cliff? Do they succeed or fail or change their minds? You could agonize over each twist in your story, trying to decide which one is more interesting or unexpected or logical. The answer may become clear when the question is: "which choice advances my theme?"

I must confess my own prejudice. Themes are more interesting to me than plots. Dozens of books already describe creating plots. So with your permission, I'll scamper through that minefield quickly.

You may notice similar patterns within effective stories. You might even be tempted to list these as things you "should" do. But writing doesn't conform to "rules." Be wary of any advice that begins, "You should ... " We all know how our internal creative ragamuffin responds to rules and the word "should." Tell him he "should" do this, or he "must" do that, and he'll stick his thumb in his mouth and sit silently in the corner. There are no rules to creating a story. It's playing, daydreaming, a game of pretend.

Still, it can't hurt to be aware of what other writers have found useful.

Most books have a main character the reader identifies with. While we're reading, we live that character's life with him. This character wants something badly because we all want something badly. Like all of us, he faces obstacles that prevent him from getting what he wants. These may be as simple as a troll guarding the castle that contains the magic stone or as complex as the fact that achieving his goal will destroy him. Perhaps he wants mutually exclusive things. His enemy may take countermeasures to thwart him. Many writers feel that the most interesting part of anyone's life is when he wants something badly and must overcome obstacles to achieve it. Think about your own life, or your parents' lives. When you describe their lives to someone, do you describe the time they were desperate to escape the war, leave their homeland, and make the arduous journey to America? Or do you talk about their current daily routine at the senior center, and the Jell-O allergy they seem to have developed? It probably depends on what you're trying to accomplish.

The character must make decisions and take action to overcome the obstacles. These obstacles may come from the nature of the thing he desires or from an opposing character. As he makes a choice and takes action, he'll discover new challenges that spring from the actions he took. Roadblocks may become increasingly formidable until he's faced with one that appears completely unbreachable. The character sinks beneath the weight of this problem until all that remains is his central characteristic that becomes his only hope. He employs his cunning, or bravery, or faith, or love, or whatever it is, and overcomes the obstacle. Or fails to overcome it.

You can spend your life fleshing out this skeleton and, if you write well, make a fine living at it. If your character is interesting and his obstacles unique, the most experienced reader will willingly follow you. Everyone wants things, we all encounter difficulties, and we usually only succeed when we make decisions and take action. These are the interesting elements of life and therefore of literature.

Many stories are variations of the basic "hero" story outlined in exquisite detail by Joseph Campbell in *Hero With a Thousand Faces*. A character is thrust onto a journey by choice or circumstance, meets a guide or prophet, passes a series of tests, learns his lesson, and reaches something of infinite value. The hero usually has a primary source of strength that is also, paradoxically, his weakness. Achilles was dipped into magic water that gave him near-invincibility. While being dipped, the water didn't touch his heel because that's where he was held. That spot made his strength possible but was also his "heroic flaw." He died when an arrow pierced his "Achilles' heel." Heroic power often gives a character a kind of pride beyond what is acceptable in less-heroic humans. This pride, which the Greeks called "hubris," makes him take risks that ultimately lead to his downfall.

You have read dozens of books that follow the hero story; they work because they mimic life. Everyone's life is a journey we did not ask for, we all meet people who guide us one way or another, and we all endure tests as we overcome obstacles in pursuit of things that have value to us. Every hero story is an analogy of our own lives.

The story itself achieves power as it reflects larger ideas we find compelling. Sometimes we discover these ideas in the process of writing the story. Other times we craft our stories to demonstrate the ideas.

Stories spring from the nature of the characters. If you create someone with a vivid personality and strong motives, then put yourself in his shoes, he'll direct the plot for you. Put Hannibal Lector in prison, place a smart empathetic lady detective outside his cell, and if you dare become him for a while, you won't have to outline the story ahead of time. He'll drag you into it. Just remember to disengage when you're done writing.

Subplots

You are John Steinbeck writing *Of Mice and Men*. You want to convey the idea that people have to clean up their own messes even if it means destroying what they love. You've decided on the story that will convey this. Now, how can you reinforce the idea?

Being Steinbeck, you consider having a smaller story run parallel to your main one, a story that mirrors your idea in some way. Your large story involves a man and his best friend, a slow-witted but well-meaning bumbler. The smaller story travels the same idea-path with a farm hand and his dog. An even smaller story involves the bumbler and his pet mouse. Spend two hours reading his tiny book to decide if it worked.

Shakespeare did this over and over again. The kings, queens, and princes act out huge serious stories. In alternating scenes, the court jester, elves, and drunks at the local bar act out parallel stories. Because they have such different flavors, a casual observer won't even notice the similarities. Often the subplot is absurd, and funny, and gives a contrasting perspective on the same theme. It's as if *NYPD Blue* and *Seinfeld* both tackled the same idea and we watched alternating scenes of the two shows. Remarkably, the central idea is conveyed with a richness that one alone could never muster.

Not everyone uses this trick. If you don't admire Shakespeare and Steinbeck, it might not be for you. Notice whether or not your favorite author does it and make up your own mind.

Obvious subplots don't work. Even people who aren't looking for literary tricks will spot it and be disappointed that they can see cards up your sleeve. Luckily, even small subtle things can be effective. A dog whining might reinforce a character's pining for his lost love, or a song cut short might subconsciously remind a reader of a life cut short.

The first few seasons of *The West Wing* employ subplots in nearly every episode in exactly the same way Shakespeare used them. To my taste, this is one of the things that elevated those episodes above other shows of the time, and also above subsequent episodes. When they changed writers, they made different artistic decisions. Classic shows like *Taxi, Star Trek, Seinfeld* and *Frasier* used the technique all the time. You probably did not watch them like a writer, you merely let them roll over you like a common consumer. To see if you like the use of subplots, watch your favorite shows and see if you can spot them. If the writing is good, you'll have to work to notice them.

Some writers include subplots that don't parallel the larger one at all. They just provide comic relief, or allow time for larger events to happen behind the scenes, or give the reader an opportunity to digest what's going on. Humans have short attention spans, and sometimes we welcome a break. Some subplots simply gives us a bigger picture, filling in details of life during the Dark Ages, or allowing us to live through an execution without killing our main character.

Illuminate your idea with the dazzling light of your plot. Fill in shadows with subplots.

If you tell us that your character is sad, we take your word for it but don't feel the sadness ourselves. This doesn't mean we're unfeeling, just that the world is full of misery and people survive by distancing themselves from it. We don't feel the desolation and hopelessness of every famine victim we read about in the paper. We note their situation but don't sink into a sympathetic depression. Mere reporting pales when compared with living their experience. If you want us to empathize, make us live the experience; don't simply file a report.

Rather than tell us your character is sad, let us see her crying as her baby dies. Let us go with her to the store to buy bullets and help her compose a final letter to her husband. As she puts the gun to her temple, you don't need to tell us she's sad. We already know.

Writing instructors convey this by saying "show, don't tell." Show us what's happening, let us live the experience with the characters; don't merely report. Telling us someone is nervous does not engage us like seeing his palms sweat, listening to him stutter and garble his sentences, then watching him forget his own name. We want to crawl inside your characters and live their lives with them, we don't want to listen to an author give us second-hand information. Don't tell us that the monster terrified the boy. Let us walk down the dark street, jump at the sound behind us, and see the drool on the beast's fangs as it leaps from the bushes. We want to be frightened ourselves. When the boy screams, we scream, too.

Margaret Atwood could have described her character in many ways by telling us about her. Instead, in *The Handmaid's Tale*, she shows us this paragraph:

> I sit at the little table, eating creamed corn with a fork. I have a fork and a spoon, but never a knife. When there's meat they cut it up for me ahead of time, as if I'm lacking manual skills or teeth. I have both, however. That's why I'm not allowed a knife.

Does she need to tell us exactly what's going on? Not really. By showing us that scene she accomplishes the same thing in a more powerful way. The same principal applies to creating empathy for a character in a bad spot. No need to describe the character's emotions in detail. Describe the situation and let us feel the emotions ourselves.

Chekov said it this way: "If you want your reader to sympathize with a character, write colder."

That is, dispassionately fix the noose around your character's neck. Notice the birds singing as the hood is placed over his head. Tie his arms behind him, feel the rope cutting into his wrists, taste the sweat he licks from his lips, notice the churning of his stomach. Listen to the pronouncement of his death sentence, and then remove the plank he's standing on.

You don't need to tell us he wishes he were elsewhere.

Tone and Pace

I once wrote a very somber book about a druid and discovered that "somber" does not come naturally to me. My characters would be performing dark rituals in a gloomy forest full of evil spells, and I'd think of a wisecrack to insert. Obviously, it would have been inappropriate, so I restrained myself rather than shatter the mood and jerk the reader out of the scene. It took me three years to complete that book and I never bothered to revise it, or submit it, or share it with my friends. At least I learned some lessons from the process.

The tone of a book depends on choice of language, sentence length, the boldness of verbs, plot, pace, and themes. Readers are most comfortable with a degree of consistency even if it means eliminating wisecracks. Tone varies just as a piece of music changes from beginning to end, but if it changes from opera to rap and then to bluegrass, only a genius could maintain his audience. For example, once readers adjust to long sentences with ornate descriptions, they will find it odd if you suddenly switch to short, punchy sentences. But there's a place for both.

Here is how Salman Rushdie writes with fairly long sentences in *Imaginary Homelands*:

> Great white sharks, killer bees, werewolves, devils, alien horrors bursting from the chests of movie spacemen: the popular culture of our fearful times has provided us with so many variations on the ancient myth of the Beast, the 'something' lurking out there that haunts us and is hunted by us, as to make it one of the defining metaphors of the age. In the jungle of the cities, we live amongst our accumulations of things behind doors garlanded with locks and chains, and find it all too easy to fear the unforeseeable, all-destroying coming of the Ogre—Charles Manson, the Ayatollah Khomeini, the Blob from Outer Space. Clearly, many of these forebodings are the product of affluence and of power. The haves and the powerful, fearing the uprising of the have-nots and the powerless, dream of them as monsters.

These sentences average almost 35 words each. Mr. Rushdie is considered a fine writer, and many people love him. Many other people love Ernest Hemingway, who used shorter sentences. Here's an excerpt from his *A Farewell to Arms*:

> That night there was a storm and I woke to hear the rain lashing the windowpanes. It was coming in the open window. Someone had knocked on the door. I went to the door very softly, not to disturb Catherine, and opened it. The barman stood there. He wore his overcoat and carried his wet hat.

This averages nine words per sentence. Would you confuse Rushdie and Hemingway? Not likely. The length of their sentences helps define their distinctive "voices." It also helps set the tone. What an easy place to start! Sentence length.

The written word evolved from the stories told around ancient fires, and on some level it's almost like we still listen to the words we read. The sound of the words, the rhythm of the language, the way the consonants crack in our inner ear – all seem to survive on the page from those smoky evenings on some pre-Ice Age savannah. Some story tellers whisper and we lean in to catch their secrets. Others shout and wave their arms. The style of presentation tells part of the story.

To take advantage of this, match your sentences to your message. The tone of your words can be a subtle analogy to the idea you're expressing. You don't need an advanced degree to decide how long you want to chatter on before you throw in a period, so that's an easy place to start. I don't advocate long sentences or short, big words or small, adjective-rich prose or spare writing. You must decide. No one element defines a style, but to sound more like Hemingway, write short sentences. If you prefer the tone of *Love in the Time of Cholera* by Gabriel Garcia Marquez in the next example, use longer sentences. I include this because it has a completely different mood than the last long-sentence example:

> At ten o'clock no decisions had been made regarding lunch because the housecleaning was not finished yet, the bedroom was not straightened, the bathroom was not scrubbed; he forgot to replace the toilet paper, change the sheets, and send the coachmen for the children, and he confused the servants' duties: he told the cook to make the beds and set the chambermaids to cooking. At eleven o'clock, when the guests were about to arrive, the chaos in the house was such that Fermina Daza resumed command, laughing out loud, not with the triumphant attitude she would have liked but shaken instead with compassion for the domestic helplessness of her husband. He was bitter as he offered the argument he always used: "Things did not go as badly for me as they would for you if you tried to cure the sick." But it was a useful lesson, and not for him alone. Over the years they both reached the same wise conclusion by different paths: it was not possible to live together in any other way, or love in any other way, and nothing in this world was more difficult than love.

This averages 48 words per sentence. One sentence of only eleven words brings down the average, and stands out: *But it was a useful lesson and not for him alone.* The professorial author had been reading an amusing incident aloud from the history text, but with that sentence he snaps his fingers as if to say, "Pay attention class. The next sentence will be on the test." The rhythm of the sentences helps creates the tone; the change in sentence length punctuates it.

We read short sentences quickly. Vivid verbs excite us and propel us along. Longer, more complex sentences containing detailed descriptions and less aggressive verbs slow us down. Therefore, when your character is sleepy and not much is happening, it will seem natural for him to notice the gentle rocking of the boat and the clouds floating across the moon as he remembers his childhood in Greece. The next day, when he leaps into his car and guns the engine, get out of his way. Gunshots startle him, he swerves. Pedestrians leap from his path, sirens wail. He grips the steering wheel tightly and floors the accelerator. Can he beat the train to the intersection? Well, maybe he can if we don't slow him down with detailed descriptions of each car he passes or distract him with a few paragraphs of philosophy.

Let the tone and pace of your words act as background music. Play them loud and fast when the action is hot. Slow them down, stretch them out, and let their calmness soothe your reader when he's whispering to the lady he loves.

Your choice of vocabulary helps set the tone. Very intelligent characters tend to speak eloquently. When describing their actions it doesn't seem odd to let your own eloquence out of its bottle a bit. Classical language and careful sentences fit the description of a painting by Rembrandt, while describing a cartoon might call for breezier colloquial jargon. Imitating Shakespeare while describing a new computer game will probably seem humorous. Or pathetic.

Human moods vary depending, in part, on the setting. In a deserted mansion deep in a foggy swamp, with strange sounds echoing through the night, we tend to feel nervous. Especially if we're alone. Especially if weird things keep happening. Readers act just like other humans in that way. They respond to the smell of a place, the lighting, the sounds. They also respond to the mood of the people around them. If everyone in your book is nervous, sooner or later the reader will be too. If characters seem cheerful, the reader will adopt that attitude too. When everyone in a room starts giggling, it's hard to stay serious.

Location is so important to some stories that we think of it as a character itself. Perhaps the evil swamp of the preceding paragraph seems like an opponent. Your hero's antagonist might be a haunted house (or maybe the Bates Motel), or the town of Stepford, or the land of Oz, or a cursed planet. Just thinking of the setting as a character can help you define the tone of the book. The setting isn't always a passive canvas for your action to play against. Sometimes you can think of it as one of the actors.

Start at the Beginning

First drafts often begin by fumbling around for a few pages. We describe the character and scene, then fill in some background. We introduce another character or two and set them all in motion. Gradually the book becomes real for us and the writing seems easier.

When you go back to revise, you may notice that the actual story doesn't begin until page 8 or page 30. This won't bother you at all. All that introductory stuff was critical to your believing the book, and some of those sentences have become your favorites. You will believe that no one could possibly understand the book without those first eight pages.

You need to throw them away.

If the story begins on page 30, your book should begin on page 30. You can fill in the background as you go, once you've hooked your reader. If you cherish some of the sentences, rescue the little darlings and move them deeper into the manuscript.

This is because reading is much different from writing. The author needs to write those preliminary pages to bring this new world to life in his own mind, but the reader doesn't need them, not yet. The reader is riding a crowded subway and wants you to transport her into an alternative life before the first stop. If you don't, she's just going to be riding a subway, thinking about that jerk she married, worrying about the pack of teenagers a few seats behind her and resenting you for everything that's wrong with her life.

Few characters are born on page one. They've led full and interesting lives before the book begins and will have many more experiences after the book closes. Your story focuses on one portion of their life and starts the first time a character actually does something important. Until someone acts, they're off-stage. Your subway reader will tolerate a bit of "it was a dark and stormy night" until a character pulls the trigger, but not much. Hook her quickly or she's gone.

Some writers try to preserve their preliminary ramblings by writing a prologue or first chapter in which something does happen. To hook you, they stick this ahead of the rambling opening section they originally wrote. This can be an annoyingly obvious ruse but it can also be effective. The trick is to create enough curiosity in the reader that she'll endure the time you take to get your characters onto the stage with all their props in place. But even a compelling prologue buys only a little time. Squander it with the same thirty pages of setup and you'll be singing to an empty room.

In real life, we meet interesting people all the time, have pleasant conversations, and do things with them long before we know their life stories. If they interest us enough, we're happy to learn more about them later. If they bore us or insult us, we won't bother. How much do you want to know about your waiter's history? He's there to bring you food, and if that works out, maybe you'll ask him a question later. Your character is there to transport me off this stinking subway. If he gets that job done, I'll consider taking the relationship to the next level. If I know more about your character's history than you know about your boyfriend's, you might consider less exposition in the first chapter or a more talkative boyfriend. People get married without knowing their spouse's darkest childhood secrets. Surely I can get through thirty pages.

In your first draft, write whatever you need to make this imaginary world real for you. When you revise, rearrange until the piece starts at the beginning.

Dialog

A transcribed conversation isn't believable dialog. If it were, anyone with a tape recorder could write brilliant plays and novels. The written illusion of conversation is quite different from what we hear around us every day. Written words carry more weight than spoken words, but require more effort to process. Dialog needs to be more concise than actual conversation, with the words chosen more carefully. We don't want to read unimportant mutterings.

Notice how we summarize conversations in life. The telephone rings – it's your father. The conversation lasts for ten minutes, but when you hang up you tell your wife, "Uncle Frank died and left me the factory." Ten minutes of dialog compressed to one sentence. If you repeated the entire phone conversation word for word, your wife would quickly become bored. Effective written dialog is similarly compressed.

In *Sweet Thursday* by John Steinbeck (the sequel to *Cannary Row*), we find an example of the relative brevity of exchanges in dialog. Hazel is a sweet and loyal man, but not the brightest firefly in the cornfield. Fauna runs a sort of "entertainment" service. She has just run an astrology chart on Hazel and doesn't want to tell him the results. Notice how short each exchange is:

.

"You got my stars wrote down?" Hazel demanded anxiously.

Fauna regarded him sorrowfully. "I don't want to tell you," she said.

"Why not? Is it bad?"

"Awful," said Fauna.

"Come on, tell me. I can take it."

Fauna sighed. "I've checked it over and over," she said. "You sure you give me your true birthday?"

"Sure."

"Then I don't see how it can be wrong." She turned wearily and faced the others. "The stars say Hazel's going to be President of the United States."

There was a shocked silence.

"I don't believe it," said Mack.

"I don't want to be President," Hazel said, and he didn't.

"There is no choice," said Fauna. "The stars have spoke. You will go to Washington."

"I don't want to!" Hazel cried. "I don't know nobody there."

"I wonder where we could all go," said Whitey No.2. "I seen some islands in the Pacific that was pretty nice. But hell, Hazel would have them too. The U.S. got a mandate."

"I won't take it," said Hazel.

Mack said, "We could kill him."

"His stars don't say it," Fauna said. "He's going to live to seventy-eight and die from a spoiled oyster."

"I don't like oysters," said Hazel.

"Maybe you'll learn in Washington."

Mack said, "Maybe you made a mistake."

"That's what I hoped," said Fauna. "I went over and over it. No, sir! Hazel is going to be President."

"Well, we've weathered some pretty bad ones," Eddie offered forlornly.

When I notice that my characters drone on for a paragraph or two at a time, I hear Steinbeck quietly clucking at me in despair. He was willing to teach me; all I had to do was pay attention while I read his books. Other writers use much longer exchanges. What does your favorite author use? If you can't answer, you're not reading like a writer yet.

Dialog brings characters to life. Agreements and disagreements identify relationships, word choices define individuals. You can tell a lot about a man, or a character, by his vocabulary and how he speaks. No need to tell the reader Mr. A is educated because his language does it for you. We deduce Mr. B's foreign heritage by his language missteps. And we know Mr. C and Mr. D have been feuding for years because we listen to them feud. The writer doesn't need to explain a thing:

> "You ain't had a original thought since 1949," said Rufus, spitting on the dirt.
> "Well, that was about the time your original idea was to swipe my prize rooster," answered Uncle Charlie. "So if stealin's what you mean by original thoughts, I guess they'll be givin' you one of them noble prizes. You been the number one original guy for fifty years."

Do we need to define the ages of these characters? No, they did it themselves in their dialog. Do we need to tell the reader they argue with each other? No, we observed them arguing. We also know they have an interest in roosters, they spit, and they mispronounce Nobel prize, so they probably don't own one. And wasn't it more fun for us to learn all that by listening to them, rather than by reading it in a long description?

Dialog is reciprocal by definition. If one character goes on too long before another responds, it will seem like a lecture or a speech. Dialog, like ping-pong, is only interesting if two people bat the thing back and forth, each adding spin according to their individual and often conflicting strategies.

In times of heightened emotion people say exactly what's on their minds; "Stop or I'll shoot," for example. No subtlety or nuance, no subcontext, no metaphorical meandering. In such times they respond directly as well: "Okay, I'll stop. Don't shoot."

But sometimes they dance around unspoken meanings and respond indirectly. Spoken words are only clues to what someone really thinks. This is counterintuitive; you won't believe it until you spy on some conversations. We decode underlying meanings so naturally we don't even notice we do it. In literature, dialog that is too literal sounds cartoonish. Authentic-sounding dialog does not always reflect what the characters actually think:

Your character comes home very late from a poker game and meets his wife.

"That must have been a fun game," she says tersely.

Do you believe she's really congratulating him on how much fun he had playing poker? No, you do not. He's about to catch Hell and we all know it. Her message lies beneath the surface of the words.

"I didn't ask you to wait up," he responds foolishly.

He does not respond to what she said, but what she meant. And he does not say what he's really thinking either, which is geez, I'm tired, can't you yell at me in the morning? Instead, he tries to redirect the conversation, and we all know it won't work. Does she respond directly to his words? Not in this lifetime she doesn't.

"I was looking forward to watching the late show with you," she says.

This has nothing to do with his last comment. It's not a response at all, plus she's not really talking about herself, or the late show. She's saying, "If you love me you would have come home earlier so you could be with me. You like your poker buddies better than you like me."

OK, that's what she thinks she means. But she really means "I'm so mad at you I could spit, and I'm going to say whatever I think will make you feel the worst." Being a man, he doesn't respond directly to either her words or her meaning, but once again tries to redirect the conversation.

"I won thirty bucks," he says sheepishly

Here's an exercise to see how well you understand dialog. Choose one of the following for the wife's response:

A) "Oh that's wonderful!" she says. "Let me make you some hot chocolate to celebrate!"

or

B) "Let me tell you exactly where you can put that thirty bucks for safe keeping."

Of course, sometimes there are good reasons for miscommunication. This is from *The Enduring Chill* by Flannery O'Conner:

> "It's so nice to have you come," Asbury said. "This place is incredibly dreary. There's no one here an intelligent person can talk to. I wonder what you think of Joyce, Father?"
>
> The priest lifted his chair and pushed closer. "You'll have to shout," he said. "Blind in one eye and deaf in one ear."
>
> "What do you think of Joyce?" Asbury said louder.
>
> "Joyce? Joyce who?" asked the priest.
>
> "James Joyce," Asbury said and laughed.
>
> The priest brushed his huge hand in the air as if he were bothered by gnats. "I haven't met him," he said. "Now. Do you say your morning and night prayers?"
>
> Asbury appeared confused. "Joyce was a great writer," he murmured, forgetting to shout.
>
> "You don't eh?" said the priest. "Well you will never learn to be good unless you pray regularly. You cannot love Jesus unless you speak to Him."
>
> "The myth of the dying god has always fascinated me," Asbury shouted, but the priest did not appear to catch it.

Characters

Every novel is populated by individuals called characters. They are the cast of your story. Usually they're humans, but not always. Short stories also have characters, and so do many news articles, essays, and even poems.

Every character is just like you in many ways; they each have an appearance, history, things they love, things they fear, things that motivate them. We don't need to know everything about them, but we do need to know enough about them to make them interesting. They need to become alive for the reader. Some people are character junkies; they don't care what happens in a book so long as they get to know the characters intimately. Your own characters will reflect the things you find important in the humans you encounter in your life. If you focus on people's appearance, you will describe your characters visually. If you think of people in terms of their resume of accomplishments, that's how you'll describe your characters. This is a little scary.

Those of us who are a bit superficial need to pretend we're interested in other people when we write characters. Imagine that you care about other people's opinions and emotions when you write so you can inject some emotion into your cast. Try to pretend you're listening when someone speaks to you, just as an experiment. You don't want all your characters to be exact copies of you, with the same hobbies, the same prejudices, the same vocabulary, the same history. Imagine how a priest feels, or a murderer, or a dolphin, when you write them. The better you are at pretending to be a character, then writing down the things you notice while in that role, the richer the population of your book.

You can take any book you like, or any movie, and figure out what made a character memorable for you. You will probably decide that they had interesting choices to make, an interesting process for making their decisions, strong conflicts to be overcome, certain admirable qualities, and flaws that made them vulnerable. Just like humans.

I like books that are populated with real people, people I feel I know, individuals I care about. Each one has a history, habits, an appearance, friends, family, a means of surviving in their world (a job, an inheritance, a business, a craft etc.). They have food preferences. They love something, they hate something, they fear something. They do things for reasons and have secret goals, dreams, and ambitions. Something in the past changed their life. Part of them remains unchanged from childhood, but not all parts. The choices they've made have cost them and molded them. They regret some of those choices. They see themselves a certain way; their friends may see them differently; their enemies certainly do. They have a strength they fall back on in times of stress: their sense of humor, their physical abilities, their logic, their wealth, or a network of friends. Strangers have an impression of them when they meet. They believe some things that other people don't. Some of their weaknesses are not obvious because they hide them. Most adults have had a defining crisis that colors their actions and attitudes.

Does the reader need to know all that? No. Some authors fill in all the blanks for us, others only provide clues. When we encounter a great, memorable character we sense that the author knows him well. We may not need to know what event made Mike Hammer the way he is, or why he deals with women the way he does, but we have no doubt Micky Spillane could tell us if we asked. We never learn much about Hamlet's childhood but sense that Shakespeare lived it with him.

Some writers slap a few superficial characteristics onto a character like a coat of cheap paint and hope readers will mistake it for art. For some kinds of books, and some characters, that's fine. But the most engrossing characters become the reader's lifelong friends because we learn important things about them and care about them. Like the rest of our friends, they aren't perfect, but there's something we admire about them.

Some characters don't rise to the level of "reader's friend." They merely serve a purpose in a book; but they still need to seem realistic. Many writers find these minor characters the most difficult. Some tricks make it easy to write more interesting minor characters.

If you can't picture a character, borrow someone. Pick a friend, a relative, an acquaintance, or even a public figure. You already know what they look and sound like, how they move, their opinions, mannerisms, and history. Give them a part to play in your book. I've done this several times, and luckily, I'm not such a good writer that anyone notices. Familiar people are easy to describe because you can see them in your mind. If you can't picture a character, your reader can't either.

For example, you might cast your book with actors. John Wayne will play the bartender, Elvis the mechanic, Madonna the receptionist. Obviously, you'll give them new names. If you're a brilliant writer it will be too obvious and you'll have to give Madonna red hair and a limp. This short cut helps you visualize the population of your story. I once used the character Kramer from *Seinfeld* and a guy I met in a bar; I haven't heard from either one of them. With billions of people on Earth, you don't necessarily need to create brand new ones for every role. As long as you stay away from your immediate family, and give everyone new costumes, you probably won't get sued. You can even name the character "Elvis" while you write the early drafts, then use your word processing program to change every "Elvis" in the book to "Rick," and no one will ever know. Maybe Rick says, "Thank you very much, ma'am" a lot, and sneers, and swivels his hips when he dances, and women love him, but unless he sings "Blue Suede Shoes," few will see past his disguise.

Some writers outline characters before writing them. They give each one a history, opinions, an appearance, a job, and a hobby. By the time they start writing, each character is an old friend and easy to describe.

Another approach is to create an analogy for each character. The policeman is a weasel, the thug is a bear, the hero is a wolf. With strong images in your mind, you'll write them consistently. If the heroine is a harp, you'll find yourself describing her in musical terms. The professor is a minivan: he's self-contained, dependable, and comfortable, with room to collect ideas for class. The investment banker is greed, or happiness, or a library; the grocery store clerk is lust, or a wheat field. What a grand game, to write about lust and greed as played by Elvis and John Malkovich. And no one will know you're doing it, because you won't tell them.

People tend to read faster once you've entranced them; they read names and other recurring words quickly. Why slow them down by creating characters or places with similar names? Why force them to read every letter in every name? If Bruce argues with Bryce at the Maybell Bar, and Mandy and Molly exchange life stories with Mindy at the Mayfly Bar, you'll have unhappy readers. You're making them work too hard. Let Everett argue with Bruce at the dump while Jane gossips with Molly at The Gentle Host Restaurant. Once up to speed, the reader will see the first letter of each name and dash merrily onward. Avoid obvious problems by giving characters names that begin with different letters.

Names convey information directly and indirectly. "Moose" creates the presumption of size, "Ginger" is spicy, "Elvis" reminds us of the singer. If you name a character "Woddy Allmen," readers will see a bespeckled New York humorist even if you want them to see an Eskimo. To convey a subconscious hint of a character's fondness for eating his fellow humans you might make his name rhyme with "cannibal." If he's very smart, you might give him a name that reminds us of a lecturing professor. Before we even meet him, our subconscious has made assumptions about Hannibal Lector.

Most readers won't notice the connection, but all will sense it. "Dirk" is an old name for a dagger. You might name a sharp, masculine character who routinely finds himself in deep holes of various kinds "Dirk Pitt." Even readers who don't know a dirk from a dirndl will sense the underlying richness from the sound alone.

Character Arc

You may hear that your character must change and grow in some way. I don't agree that he *must*.

Sure, it seems a waste of time to run your hero through the maze of your plot only to have him come out the other side untouched by his ordeal. We like it when characters grow. We love it when the bad guy sees the light and reforms. A character's growth in enlightenment mirrors the effect we'd like in our reader; it's another type of analogy. If a character's growth would reinforce your central idea, you're just lazy if you don't make him grow. Some books suggest you chart growth as an arc on a graph. Instead, I suggest you notice what your favorite author does and emulate them. Most of the time, it's probably a good idea to have your main character grow along the lines of your larger theme.

But not always.

In some stories, the character's development isn't important. Your detective analyzes clues, gets distracted by the pretty widow, manages to escape from the building before it explodes, and finally nabs the murderer. He doesn't change much, nor does he need to. In the sequel, he'll be the same guy. You'd think characters on a TV comedy would learn unforgettable lessons with each episode, but they don't. Week after week they make the same mistakes and are forced by their personalities to extricate themselves in similar ways. If they did learn and grow, they'd stop doing the absurd things that are the reasons we watch them.

Secondary characters can represent some human characteristic, like anger or kindness. That's their role in the story whether you realize it or not, and if they evolve too much, that characteristic disappears. Ebeneezer Scrooge grows over the course of *A Christmas Carol*. But if he were a secondary character in *Tiny Tim: The Early Years* he might represent greed. Who would be the foil for the kindly schoolteacher who represents altruism if we let Scrooge evolve into a jovial gentleman? Both characters must remain one dimensional while we play out the larger themes of Tiny Tim.

Sometimes a story reveals a character's suppressed characteristics. He didn't develop into a serial killer, he just resisted his evil impulses until you put the gun in his hand. That's not really a change. He was a bully since childhood, he just never had the power to act on it. Maybe Darth Vader becomes good at the end of *The Return of the Jedi* when he turns to battle his boss, the evil Emperor. But maybe his spark of goodness was there all the time, it merely emerged in that scene. It's a fine point, but noticing that distinction may be useful. Does Frodo evolve over the *Lord of the Rings*, or was it vital that his essential innocence survive without much change? There isn't one correct answer. Simply considering the issue of character development will enrich your story. Do what you want, just don't do it accidentally.

If your book deals with the idea that "sometimes you have to trust someone," and your main character can't trust anyone, you have a wonderful opportunity to illustrate your theme. His mistrustful nature gets him deeper and deeper in trouble until the only solution is for him to trust someone. If he does learn his lesson, he trusts them and grows, you've reinforced your point. If he fails to learn his lesson and Godzilla eats him, your point is still made. But if he finally trusts someone and Godzilla still eats him, what in the world were you thinking? Your message has become "trust no one: disregard what I've preached at you for three hundred pages."

Sometimes character growth makes sense, and sometimes it doesn't.

Point of View

Whose life are we living while we read your story? That's the central question of point of view. To confuse beginning writers, the term is used to describe both a mechanical technique and a story telling technique, and they're different birds. The mechanical technique is just grammar: *I ran* is grammatically "first person;" *you ran* is "second person," *he ran* is "third person."

Most writing is done from the "third person" point of view. The narrator (you) describes characters and events as an observer. Even the main character is seen from this viewpoint. "Detective Richards stepped from the shadows and picked up the gun." This is a matter of grammatical housekeeping; inconsistency with the point of view confuses your reader. We can easily live Detective Richards's life with him in the third person point of view. We'll identify with him and imagine ourselves to be him. We won't even notice that, grammatically speaking, the author is using the third person perspective.

Some folks prefer to write in the "first person." The writer pretends to be the main character, Detective Richards: "I stepped from the shadows and picked up the gun." We can live the good detective's life with him in the first person just as easily as third person, and many authors believe it's more compelling.

A few people have written books in the second person. They imagine that the reader is his main character: "You stepped from the shadows and picked up the gun." When you write a letter you may shift from first person to second: "I went to the doctor today. By the way, how was your doctor visit?" It's clear who I am, and who you are, so it doesn't bother us.

Sherman Alexie shifts to second person point of view, as if writing a letter, from time to time. This is from "Imagining the Reservation," a short story in his book *The Lone Ranger and Tonto Fistfight in Heaven*:

There are so many possibilities in the reservation 7-11, so many methods of survival. Imagine every Skin on the reservation is the new lead guitarist for the Rolling Stones, on the cover of a rock-and-roll magazine. Imagine forgiveness is sold 2 for 1. Imagine every Indian is a video game with braids. Do you believe laughter can save us? All I know is that I count coyotes to help me sleep. Didn't you know? Imagination is the politics of dreams; imagination turns every word into a bottle rocket. Adrian, imagine every day is Independence Day and save us from traveling the river changed; save us from hitchhiking the long road home. Imagine and escape. Imagine that your own shadow on the wall is a perfect door. Imagine a song stronger than penicillin. Imagine a spring with water that mends broken bones. Imagine a drum which wraps itself around your heart. Imagine a story that puts wood in the fireplace.

Changing point of view can create a cool effect like that, but it also tends to jar the reader. If Detective Richards steps from the shadows and then I pick up a gun, and then you shoot it, none of us is sure what's going on. Good writers only confuse us on purpose.

Regardless of the technical point of view, we usually focus on one or two characters and see the world through their eyes. To the storyteller, "point of view" means, "Whose life will the reader live?" Whoever it is, and regardless of whether we're grammatically in first or third person, usually we know only what they know. If I'm living the life of a blind main character, and the author keeps describing things visually, I'm not going to get an authentic experience. Simply reminding yourself whose life you want the reader to live will fix point of view problems. Put yourself into their life and then write it.

Beginning writers sometimes inadvertently snatch the reader from one life and thrust him into a different one.

You want the reader to live Detective Richards's life with him, so you let us see only what he sees and know only what he knows. Richards doesn't know there's a bomb in the building, but you, the author, can see it there on your outline. Treat it as a secret. If I hear the thoughts of his partner, Detective Richards and I are both psychics whether you want us to be or not.

Hearing a character's thoughts involves the reader in an intimate way, even if they aren't written in a dialog format, like: "I need to lose weight," she thought. This is from *Paris Trout* by Peter Dexter:

> What she could not imagine doing was calling Mr. Trout and telling him that she wasn't coming in. She was afraid how he would take it. She could not imagine herself acknowledging that what had happened the night before was out of the ordinary.
>
> And in the end, lacking imagination, she got up, attached her leg, dressed, and brushed her hair. She tried not to think about the way he had looked holding the gun, she tried not to think about the way he had looked when he smiled.
>
> In the end what she thought about was that a peg-legged woman was fortunate to have any job at all.

Some writers adopt an "omniscient third person" point of view. They let the reader hear everyone's thoughts and see the terrorists sneaking into the building before the main character knows about them. This demands delicate balance. Readers love to know secrets. They also want to live someone's life and it tires them to jump into a new life.

Some books change points of view in alternating chapters. To make it work, stay within a single point of view for a satisfyingly long time.

Some books let us hear the most important thoughts of anyone in the room. *Dune* is such a book, and it sold millions of copies. When Frank Herbert wrote it, he rose to the challenge and maintained this style throughout the book. It seems unnerving until you get used to it, but he wrote so well we finally accept it. There's nothing wrong with such an attempt, especially if you write like Herbert, but I suggest you save the experiment for your second book.

It's difficult to write dialog where more than two people speak. It just gets confusing. More than three is impossible; ask anyone. And we're supposed to stay in one character's point of view, right? Absolutely, but that's only on Planet Earth. Here's an example of how dialog goes on the planet Dune. It may help you to know the book is mostly in Paul's point of view. Jessica is his mother and a witch. Thoughts are in italics. The following section may excite you to the possibilities of multiple points of view, or it may convince you never to stray there:

> The smuggler lurched to his feet, lifted his flagon. "I'll give you a toast," he said. "To young Paul Atreides, still a lad by his looks, but a man by his actions."
>
> *Why do they intrude?* Jessica asked herself.
>
> The banker stared now at Kynes, and Jessica saw terror return to the agent's face.
>
> People began responding all around the table.
>
> *Where Kynes leads, people follow*, Jessica thought. *He has told us he sides with Paul. What's the secret of his power? It can't be because he's Judge of the Change. That's temporary. And certainly not because he's a civil servant.*
>
> She removed her hand from the crysknife hilt, lifted her flagon to Kynes, who responded in kind.
>
> Only Paul and the banker—(*Soo-Soo! What an idiotic nickname!* Jessica thought.)—remained empty handed. The banker's attention stayed fixed on Kynes. Paul stared at his plate.
>
> *I was handling it correctly*, Paul thought. *Why do they interfere?* He glanced covertly at the male guests nearest him. *Prepare for violence? From whom? Certainly not from that banker fellow.*
>
> Halleck stirred, spoke as though to no one in particular, directing his words over the heads of the guests

across from him: "In our society, people shouldn't be quick to take offense. It's frequently suicidal." He looked at the stillsuit manufacturer's daughter beside him. "Don't you think so, miss?"

"Oh, yes. Indeed I do," she said. "There's too much violence. It makes me sick. And lots of times no offense is meant, but people die anyway. It doesn't make sense."

"Indeed it doesn't," Halleck said.

Jessica saw the near perfection of the girl's act, realized: *That empty-headed little female is not an empty-headed female.*

If you gave that to your English teacher, you would get it back with many red marks. I can't count all the broken "rules." Some people find *Dune* so confusing they throw the book against the wall. Millions of others find it so exciting and different they become hooked for life.

In real life, we don't get to hear any thoughts but our own. We don't know when other people decide to do something unless they tell us they've decided. We don't know what they feel except as we interpret what they do. An omniscient writer does know these things, of course, and may tell us if she wishes. But each time I'm learning things your main character can't know, I'm no longer living his life. I've been extracted. Be careful.

Most upsetting is when I'm firmly entrenched within a character and the writer inserts a sentence or two that pulls me out, then tries to put me back. I'm having dinner with a beautiful woman, thinking my own thoughts, wondering if my lies are working. Suddenly I hear her thinking that I'm interesting and she'd always found astronauts intriguing. I stop in mid-lie and marvel at my own cleverness. If you try to put me back inside the male character's non-psychic head, I won't want to go.

Readers are adventurous and will play whatever game you give them. Just don't change the rules once they're playing, unless you really want to and think the effect is cool. If you're going to become Frank Herbert, I don't want to stop you. I want you to remember me and buy me a car.

You know that the wine bottle is full of vinegar. Your reader knows too, because he watched the cook fill it when the vinegar bottle cracked. But your hero and the woman he's convinced to join him in a glass of wine are about to get a surprise. The reader feels almost like the author, a true insider in this little world, because he knows things that even characters living the story don't know. Everyone loves to feel smarter than the character.

They also love feeling smarter than the author. For most of us, that's not such a tough trick to pull off. Imagine this story:

A clown picked up an old coin and, a few minutes later, realized he could hear other people's thoughts. He didn't know where this strange power came from, and it frightened him. He ran to a church to pray for relief from this curse. To add sincerity to his prayer, he left the coin in the poor box. When he left the church, he realized his prayers had been answered: he could no longer read other people's thoughts.

Did the author explain where this power came from or why it left? He did not. He had not apparently figured it out yet. But the reader did and felt smart.

Back in the church, a priest collects money from the prayer box and approaches the confessional. The author has a decision to make. Should the priest pick up the coin and remark, "Oh boy, it's an ancient thought-reading coin! I'm going to take this into the confessional with me. Maybe that serial killer the police are looking for will decide to wander in!"

Probably not. Let the reader be an active participant. Give him the illusion that he's smarter than you are. Have confidence in him and resist over-explaining. Treat him like an equal; if you'd catch on, so will he.

Leave Room for the Reader's Imagination

Reading is a cooperative, interactive activity. Your reader has a good imagination, and you don't need to fill in every detail for her. She doesn't want to be dragged through your story, she wants to be led through her own daydream. Sometimes, she just wants you to point the way and give her permission to decorate to her own taste. The man of her dreams may not throw his socks on the floor, leave the toilet seat up, talk with his mouth full, drive too fast, and curse a lot. If those characteristics aren't critical to a character, why spoil her fun? Leave room for her imagination.

Conflict

Conflict fascinates people. We watch football games, bar fights, and hostile takeovers because they involve conflict. In books, the murderer wants to escape, the detective wants to arrest him. Without those opposing motives, it's a newspaper story from a thousand miles away.

Daily human life is a kaleidoscope of conflicts that prevent us from becoming bored and jaded. Most lives involve relatively small conflicts: I want to lose weight, but I want that pie even more. A perfectly realistic book could be constructed of comfortable characters who are indecisive, inactive, and ineffective. At least a perfectly realistic book about my life could be. But no one wants to live a jaded character's boring life. Give us conflict.

You feel that your story brims with conflict, but you may be fooling yourself. To make sure, take a sheet of paper and outline the conflicts. The murderer wants to escape, the detective wants to nab him. Plenty of conflict, right?

Wrong. The struggle may be implied, but we only feel a sense of conflict as the murderer takes actions to thwart the detective and the detective overcomes them. If I say, "Gee, I'd like to lose weight, but what the heck ... " as I eat some pie, we don't believe that my expressed conflict was real. My actions don't reveal any serious struggle. On the other hand, if my dedication to diet compels me to give the pie away, then I change my mind and break into my friend's house and steal it back, then repent and lock the purloined pie in my safe and throw the key into the well, but then climb down the well to retrieve the key, we may decide that I'm having an internal conflict. Simply posting a note on my refrigerator saying "Don't eat pie" won't do it.

Conflict implies choices and decisions. When you've finished your book, make a list of all the choices your characters agonized over, the decisions they made, and the actions they took. If the conflict is between two characters, list both their choices and how each responded to the other's moves. If your main character is the only one employing strategies, he's practicing tennis strokes against a brick wall. Your kind friends will say something like, "I liked the story, but it failed to fully engage me." If the bad guy never actually does anything, he's not much of a nemesis, he's a theoretical enemy. If the hero never has conflicting desires and choices to make that lead to actions with consequences, he's a cardboard character.

Reflection vs. Action

Our lives consist of a series of bright shining moments interrupted by hours of staring out the window. When historians write about our lives, they'll edit out most of those hours of staring out the window.

Good books imitate life. Some scenes are full of action, conflict, and decision. In more reflective scenes, the narrator tries to make sense of it all. Many good books alternate action scenes with reflective scenes according to their own internal rhythm. Reflective scenes give the reader an opportunity to make sense of it all as well. If you don't give her this opportunity, the book will seem cartoonish.

On the other hand, if your book contains nothing but scenes of reflection, you better hope the writing is so lucid and uplifting that English literature professors will love it for its language, categorize it "literary fiction," and hire you to teach creative writing. Your work will be praised within that inner circle of university-based authors and thirty copies will be sold.

If that's the direction your muse leads, by all means follow her. Your muse may not be Bart Simpson, your inner editor may not be Colonel Klink. Thirty copies sold to adoring fans who truly understand you is nothing to sneeze at. That would be a wildly successful life.

Perhaps, like Stephen King, none of us has a choice. We write what we must write.

Improving

Practice

When I like an author, I tend to read several of her books. Often, this means seeking out her earlier works. The more I do this, the more convinced I become that writing skill comes from practice, not talent.

I love John Steinbeck. After reading his most famous books, I sought out his first books. Without knowing you, I'm confident you can already write as well as he could when he wrote them. They contain none of the soaring eloquence or insight of his later books. Had I been an editor, I would have rejected my hero, perhaps with a sarcastic note designed to discourage him from writing anything else. I was disappointed and embarrassed by his clumsiness. Upon reflection, I decided the proper response was to feel encouraged. If he could improve as much as he did, there's hope for me.

Some writers move the opposite direction. I love their first book and become increasingly disenchanted with each subsequent book until finally, sadly, I stop reading them.

Clearly, writers can improve with practice, yet not all do. But why? I haven't thought of a gracious way to ask an author why they let themselves go to seed, why they discarded the enormous gift they displayed in their earlier work. So I used deductive reasoning to come up with an explanation.

We all know people who have played an instrument for a long time without improving much. Many of us play golf or other sports and never get better. The reason is that we never consider our craft critically and actually try to improve. Writing is like that.

If you consciously look for weaknesses in your guitar playing, then practice the troublesome fingering over and over, pretty soon the weakness disappears. Perhaps you try playing with a metronome to discover passages you tend to rush or slow. You may find a teacher to point out things you don't notice, or to teach you new tricks. There's nothing wrong with playing the same three chords and ten songs for your whole life, of course, if you enjoy doing it. On the other hand, don't be bitter if no one wants to buy your CD. You haven't actually concentrated on elevating your skill, and we can all hear it. If you want to improve, you have to actually try to improve. On behalf of all your long-suffering friends, please, buy a metronome, take some lessons.

Some people sell a book for big money early in their career. From then on, no one wants to be too critical. Editors are reluctant to interfere with a proven cash cow. Friends don't want to risk your tantrum by being too honest. Your fragile ego is reassured by your success: look at the car I drive, you think – obviously I'm a great writer. Why look for flaws?

Other people are never satisfied. They revise a sentence twenty times, honing it toward perfection. They practice for hours, but their goal isn't merely to write more words but to write better words.

I once had breakfast with a man who'd published more than fifty books using several pseudonyms. He made a good living and had learned to churn out books quickly. He had contracts for several more books, and these kept him busy. As we finished our coffee, he looked off into the distance and softly said, "Some day I'd like to try and write a really good book." The comment startled me. I couldn't help but wonder why he didn't try to make each book a good book but I didn't say anything. With his schedule, he didn't have time to be critical, to seek flaws and revise several times. He had to write twenty pages today. He didn't have time to focus on improving and he knew that, until he did, he'd be confined to producing workmanlike books that would not survive him. Good books but not great books. Temporary books.

Luckily, you and I don't have this problem. We ain't even that good yet.

To release your creativity, practice slapping words onto paper without being critical. To improve your craft, practice revising critically with the conscious goal of improving. Look for flaws and fix them.

Read books on writing and experiment with their suggestions. Subscribe to writing magazines, invite other writers to criticize your work. Read your creation out loud and see if you like the way it sounds. Attend conferences, take classes, write poetry, play with writing in new styles and genres. See if you can imitate the style of people you admire, and even of people you don't admire. Join a critique group and look for your own weaknesses in other people's work.

I hope that doesn't sound like drudgery, because it's not. Writing anything is fun, the way making a ceramic teapot is fun. Even more fun is continuing to shape it until it's beautiful. But no experience can match the feeling of polishing it until a genie emerges to hover above you.

Critique Groups

Believe it or not, you're not the only writer living in your community; sooner or later you'll want to find the others. When you do, you'll discover that you belong to a family you never knew existed. They will welcome you, and some will become close friends. They may introduce you to editors and agents, recommend books, and help you in dozens of ways. Some day, you'll do the same for others. The reference librarian at your public library may be able to direct you toward other writers. The book editor of your newspaper or community relations person at your favorite bookstore may be able to help. Many local writing groups maintain websites. On a search engine like google.com, enter your city and words like writer, author, critique, and publisher.

If six writers live in a community, they probably assemble once a month to read and comment on each other's work. These critique groups can be valuable, rewarding, and more fun than Disneyland.

The primary benefit is mutual support. Writing is a solitary sport, and it's easy to lose confidence. You will doubt you're engaged in a worthy pursuit. Without knowledgeable readers, you'll doubt your skill and question your progress. You'll feel lonely.

If you join or create a writers' group, remember that the other members joined for the same reasons. They want support and encouragement as much as they want criticism. If you brutalize their work they will stick pins into little dolls that look like you. And, of course, you'll prejudice their reactions to your own words.

Beyond support, writers' groups provide some things you can't get any other way. It's easy to get caught up in a well-crafted story. Once enthralled, it's hard to step back and identify the author's techniques. It's much easier in a less-polished work. Luckily, most people bring less-polished work to their group and flaws will leap out at you. Certainly, if you can gently point these out, you'll do the writer a favor. Much more valuable is noticing a weakness and realizing you commit the same sin. Your stylistic trick of changing point of view exactly eight times per page always seemed bold and creative to you. When another writer does it and you gag, you may reconsider. Other writers can act as a kind of mirror for you: read their words to see your own mistakes.

One small warning. The most experienced authors still feel vulnerable about their work and will expand the meaning of each negative comment to about six times its intended size. When you say a sentence is "fine," meaning only that you can't think of a more cogent comment, they will hear, "It's dull and ordinary and not worthy of its paper." If you say you didn't like a character, they hear that you despise the book, hate their mother, and revile the car they drove to the meeting. Understate your negative comments so that, when this happens, criticisms swell only to their intended size. It's also wise not to pick on details, or punctuation and grammar errors. Fifteen typos doesn't mean it's a bad chapter, just that it needs proofreading. But fifteen negative comments can kill all the fun of a writing project.

It's much easier to see flaws than strengths but observing little successes is equally valuable. You can learn from the brief flashes the worst writer exhibits. Find and compliment those flashes. If you can't think of anything else, compliment the writer's typing or choice of good clean white paper, or their ambition at even trying to take on such a difficult writing project. This will temper the writer's reaction to your criticisms, make him feel good, and reassure him that you don't hate him personally. It's not dishonest, it's just common civility.

Remember all this when it's your turn to receive comments. Your friends have not read this book and simply don't know any better. Try not to react to their clumsy attempts to help you; they did not mean to sound as piercingly negative as they do. Most important, don't argue. They'll only argue back. Don't justify your writing or explain why you made the choices you did. When your work makes it to the marketplace, you won't have that opportunity. The words you wrote will have to flare or fizzle on their own.

In that respect, the reader is always right. If something confused him, you'll never convince him that he's merely too stupid to appreciate your art. It *did* confuse him, and maybe you can improve it so it won't. If he's actually just too stupid, the most persuasive argument won't make him smarter. The best plan is to suggest he buy this book. Just because he can't help you doesn't mean he can't help me.

Some people get more pleasure from finding fault than they do by being constructive. Your group will have at least one such person and there's no benefit to ruining his fun. Thank him for his insightful comments, take them for what they're worth and move on. Don't retaliate when you read his work. It won't make you a better writer, and that's why you're there.

Never ever direct your comments toward the author herself. Always focus on the words on the page, what you like as well as whatdoesn't resonate as strongly within you. Don't say, "you always do this." That's directed at the person. Say, "This reminds me of that thing you wrote last month." Don't say, "Here's what you must do to fix this problem." Say, "I wonder what would happen if this character did this?" They don't want you to "fix" their work. They don't want you to write for them, they want your reaction to what they've written.

If you bristled at my telling you "don't do this" in the preceding paragraph, you understand my point. I don't even know you yet you're taking my comments personally. Remember that reaction when you tell someone else what to do to fix their writing.

Weigh each criticism and choose which ones deserve attention. People focus on different things, some important and some trivial. Plus, taste varies and you can't please everyone. Make whatever changes you want, if any, but don't think you have to do anything your group suggests. This may drive your friends crazy, but it's your project. J.R.R. Tolkien belonged to a critique group called

"The Inklings" that included several excellent writers, including C.S. Lewis. Tolkien loved the group, never missed a meeting, and smoked his pipe cheerfully as they made suggestions for *The Hobbit*. To the consternation of his group, he never took a single suggestion to heart, never made a change they wanted. He just liked hanging out with the group.

When it's your turn to comment, resist making trivial complaints and share important observations as gently as possible.

If you don't enjoy your group and don't feel it's useful to you, leave it. You can always find or create another. The writing process is fun, but so is the experience of being read. A good critique group can provide that fun. But a bad group, a group you don't enjoy, isn't worth anything.

Journals

The scene you're about to write intimidates you. Perhaps it's an important love scene that must be tender and gentle and come from your heart. Unfortunately, this morning you had a fight with your spouse, the landlord handed you an eviction notice, and you just hung up from arguing with an unreasonable bill collector. You're having a little trouble getting into a romantic mood.

Before you write the love scene, try writing a page or two about your own life. Write about the fight with your spouse, the landlord, and the bill collector. Release your stress by translating it into words.

Obviously, you're not going to show that page to anyone. You're writing it for yourself, so write quickly and badly. Don't fuss over it. Once you've dissipated the emotions and processed your thoughts, you can return to the more interesting task at hand.

Many writers find that the first writing of any day is weaker than what they produce later in the day. It's too influenced by reality. To counter this, they keep a journal and write in it as a limbering-up exercise. John Steinbeck began each day by writing a few pages about his own life and the next scene he intended to write. While journaling, he transitioned from his real life to his writing life without creating more words that needed later revision. Two of these journals have been published.

Being a somewhat lazy writer myself, while writing one book, rather than keep my own journal, I used his. I read a few pages of his journal each day before writing. Do what works for you. If the first words each day seem the hardest or the least graceful, try keeping a journal. It's a way of warming up your muse, or in my case, letting Bart Simpson loosen his arm by throwing a few paper airplanes from the back of the class before turning him loose on an important water balloon project.

Making Notes

Many people keep a little pad of paper (or electronic organizer) with them at all times. When an idea springs out of an alleyway, or a great phrase pounces from a trashcan, they capture the little bugger before it can slither away. The creatures rarely attack when you sit down to write, knowing they are safest far from your Ritual Place of Creating. Most of the great ideas and fine images have escaped in this way, and they're out there waiting for you. If you're always armed, you become the hunter rather than the prey.

You'll know you've been victimized when you say, "I thought of a perfect line, but now I can't remember it."

Poetry

Writing poetry is fun. For some people, it's the white-water rafting of the writing adventure. Paradoxically, reading other people's poetry can be a dismal punishment. Millions of people write poetry but only eight people actually buy poetry books. Luckily, you can ignore those eight readers because they only buy each other's poetry anyway. Write what you want to write; forget the "market" and anyone else's opinion. There is no correct way to create poetry.

Poetry is language stripped of all rules and conventions except the ones you choose. Don't like punctuation, grammar, and capital letters? Leave 'em out, like ee cummings did. Can't be bothered with little words like "the," "a," or "is?" Skip 'em. Don't like rhyme or meter? Ignore them. Don't like complete sentences? No problem. Use them or not. If you merely want to create a list of words that have some meaning for you, feel free to do so:

> payday – insufficient;
> dreams – better;
> Sleep.

I just made that up this minute, and I feel better already.

It's liberating to string together powerful words and interesting images outside the structure of narrative. Writing poetry is a victimless pastime unless you force someone to read it. Poems don't need to "mean" anything or be consistent or beautiful. Let's face it, they're just words. If you want other people to love your words you'll have to work harder, but that's a whole different process.

Just write down the first word or image that jumps into your mind, then the next one and so forth. Stop whenever you like. The reason a sane person like yourself might commit poetry is that it goes beyond forcing your internal editor to sit in the closet – it sends him to Switzerland. There's nothing for a grownup to do when the job at hand is to "make a mess in the mud." If you ever feel like writing's not fun, that it has miraculously become work and the words won't come, write some poetry, and define poetry however you like. Your brain constantly buzzes with words and images; just write them down in a random fashion. The goal is not to write excellent verse, it's to practice getting out of your own way. At some point you'll find that pointy-headed phrases spring from you with little provocation even if you'd rather they didn't. Then, when you need a unicorn for some sentence, it won't be as hard to capture one.

That's one way to look at poetry, a warm-up exercise for Real Writing.

Another view holds that poetry itself is a valuable art form, and I subscribe to this opinion. I spit out poetry fairly often. Some idea or image pops into my brain unbidden and I scribble out six lines, or twenty. Several dozen of these little buggers have actually been published, and earned me maybe twenty bucks total. Mostly I don't submit them, or even show them to anyone. They go directly from my brain to the back of a napkin or a used envelope, and then into a big cardboard box under a table in my office.

A reasonable person would ask why I bother. But in this respect, I am not a reasonable person; I don't ask why, I just do it. Perhaps it's a way of honoring that mysterious muse that also gives me wisecracks and guides me when I struggle to explain calculus or electronics in clear language. When the muse knocks on my door, I invite her in so she understands she's always welcome.

Another confession: I love to read poetry, and try to read some every day. Call me a geek, but fine poetry touches me in a way nothing else can.

Poetry, like music and art, communicates on a deeper level than words: you can't recreate the experience by using sentences. It doesn't matter what a poem "means." You can't paraphrase a poem "in other words" without destroying the experience itself and it's silly to try. When ee cummings says "not even the rain has such small hands" there is no way to translate that. Yet it feels like it means something, it isn't gibberish.

A poem is a painting, words brushed onto a page. It reflects the poet and his relationship with the parts of reality no one understands. Like a painting, it also reflects the reader, a kind of mirror.

To accomplish this cosmic magic, the poet must distract the Colonel Klink/editor within himself. Simply telling him to wait in the closet isn't enough, we need him in a different time zone. Therefore, we force him to play complex games that have little to do with inspiration. The game can be as simple as telling him to make sure the lines rhyme. If we start with "Roses are red, violets are blue..." Klink starts churning out rhymes like a computer: zoo, flue, rue, sluice, goo, hue, eschew, Timbuktu, Kalamazoo, fondue ... and while he's occupied, our muse provides the missing words.

If Klink catches on to that game, we give him a more complex one. For example, every line must have so many "beats" and a certain rhythm: "Roses are red/violets are blue" has two beats per line, if you think of it like music and tap your foot:

RO-ses are RED

VIOLETS are BLUE.

That's "2/2 time" in musical terms, just like a march. The lines of a poem are labeled according to the way they rhyme (A rhymes with A, B with B, etc.) In a typical "Roses are red" poem, the rhyme scheme goes A, B, C, B. That is, the second and fourth lines rhyme, the other two don't. This game has both rhyme and meter (the beat in poetry is called the meter). Perhaps this will occupy Klink and he won't notice if our muse sneaks in with some fresh muddy ideas. For example, "Sugar is sweet/And so are you." But sooner or later Klink may figure out the game and start editing while you try to invite inspiration. So we make the game even more complex:

The lines of limericks have these beats: 3, 3, 2, 2, 3.

And this rhyming scheme: A, A, B, B, A.

While you write a limerick, Klink has to busy himself keeping track of the beats in each line, as well as the rhyme scheme. Here's an example of a limerick:

There once was a poet name cummings

Whose poems were all very cunning

He shunned punctuation

And capitalization

And I sure wish that I could become him.

Okay, that's not a perfect example of rhyming, or beat for that matter, but you know enough limericks you can try it yourself. On the other hand, I wrote that this moment in hopes of coming up with a good example and while my own Klink was thinking of rhymes for cummings the rest of the words stumbled out of me. So, maybe it's a good example after all, and I'll leave it in.

When Klink gets good at limericks he starts to edit while you create. So you make him juggle more pieces. Now perhaps every line must have four beats or eight beats:

> Once upon a midnight dreary
> while I pondered, weak and weary.

Many poets and songwriters spend a lifetime in the world of four beat (and eight beat) poems. Perhaps ninety percent of modern music is in four beats. But hundreds of years ago, when poetry was respectable, the Klinks of the age mastered four beats, so poets graduated to five beats per line, or "pentameter." In music this is the equivalent of 5/4 time, used by Dave Brubeck in "Take Five" or in the theme to Mission Impossible. Our ears are not accustomed to five beats per line and it sounds pretty jazzy to us, and even weird. But 400 years ago, this was the hot rhythm for poetry. They made rules about the rhythm of the words within the beat. For example, the ever-popular "iambic" rhythm goes like this; "duh-DAH." Five iambic beats per line made up "iambic pentameter:"

Duh-DAH duh-DAH duh-DAH duh-DAH duh-DAH

When well-trained Elizabethan Klinks could juggle iambic pentameter with ease, poets created forms requiring specific numbers of lines and rhyme schemes. The sonnet required precisely thirteen lines, for example, in iambic pentameter, and various varieties of sonnets had different rhyme schemes. The "Shakespearian sonnet" does not refer exclusively to a poem by William Shakespeare, although it's named after him. It refers to a thirteen line poem in iambic pentameter with a specific kind of rhyme scheme which I would tell you if I could remember it.

The point is, poets created fabulously complex and specific games to occupy the logical editorial portion of their brains, leaving the front door wide open for any stray muse to wander through. Feel free to learn any of these forms or create your own if it feels useful to you.

But the magic of poetry resides in the words themselves, not the form. It isn't necessary to use elaborate rules, or any rules at all, to paint poetry onto a page. Just open the door when your own muse knocks.

Write Your Own Rules

Some people outline every detail of a story or article before they write the first word, some have no idea where a story will take them. Some love long flowery sentences, others prefer short incisive ones. Some write with a pencil, others prefer a computer. Try different strategies until you discover what works for you. There are no correct procedures, including the suggestions I've made. For every "rule" you learn, you'll find a writer who ignores it and yet produces compelling art. The one consistent characteristic of effective writers seems to be this: at some point they become conscious of their own preferences and seek to incorporate them. They read critically, notice what they like, and shamelessly use the tricks they discover.

You can devise your own rules for writing as you read, as you drive, as you ride on the train. Many people like the structure of a game-plan to work from. Will you just start writing or will you start by outlining a story? Whose style of writing resonates with you and why? What tricks of the trade can you steal from them?

Finishing

Publishing is not the same as writing. Many people write fine work that is never published. Historically, a writer sent his manuscript off to a publishing company in New York and waited to learn if he would be accepted into the world of "real writers." Today's writers have more options. Self-publishing has become a huge industry; electronic books and "print on demand" books are becoming more prevalent. Certainly the Internet created a vast new model for publishing: write something and publish it on your own website.

In many ways it's a glorious time to write. No one can prevent you from publishing your words. But you still have a better shot of developing a following if you write well, rewrite mercilessly, and edit vigorously. That is, finish your work. Make it as good as you can before you unleash it on the world.

If you want someone else to publish your words, dozens of books will advise you. I'll just mention one trap to avoid because it comes up frequently.

Publishers often want to see a proposal and writing sample rather than a completed book or article. They can tell from this tidbit if a project interests them. This policy sometimes tempts writers to finish a work only after it's sold.

This is efficient for established writers. You've got ideas for six books or articles, you've proven that you can finish what you start, and there's no question about your craftsmanship. You choose to write the one that sells.

But until you have a track record, even knowing about this policy gets in your way. One writer I know had an idea for a book, wrote a few chapters, and started submitting it. Two years later he hadn't sold it, nor had he finished the book. He refused to spend energy writing the book until some publisher wrote him a check. During that time he could have finished that book, revised it, and written another. Unfortunately for my example, in his case, the strategy worked. He sold the book and then wrote it, but he missed out on two years of letting himself write, two years of practice. It's like saying "I won't walk on the beach until someone hires me to walk on the beach." That feels like excessive artistic integrity to me.

When you go back to revise a first draft, you may be surprised at how the project has changed since you began. New characters have sprung to life, the plot has twisted in ways you didn't predict, and you discover important themes lurking below your literal story. The synopsis you started with no longer applies. If you've already sold the book based on that synopsis, you're stuck, and may have to abandon all your improvements. You might realize that the actual story begins on page 21 and decide to discard the first twenty pages, or integrate them into later chapters. How will you feel if those are the pages you submitted? In its new form, it's perfect for a particular publisher. But that publisher already rejected it (based on pages that are no longer part of the book), so they won't consider it again.

Alternatively, you might sell it based on a sample. When you rewrite, the true beauty of your idea reveals itself to you and you realize it must be set in ancient Greece rather than Cleveland. Tough luck, buddy. The masterpiece that now aches to be written must be postponed. You've got a contract. You're gonna be in Cleveland for a while.

My advice: finish your projects before you try to sell them.

Nonfiction

Explaining, teaching, and reporting resemble telling a good story in more ways than you'd imagine. Active verbs still express ideas more vigorously than passive ones, the narrator maintains a certain point of view, and precise words increase efficiency. Unnecessary words and unimportant details clutter the page, conflicts drive events, emotion drives the reader. Nonfiction articles often involve people, and people are just three-dimensional characters who can sue you if you lie about them. Our senses place us in the scene, ambiguity distracts us.

But in nonfiction the writer must consider who the reader is and what he knows. You'd slant an article on DNA differently for Ph.D. biologists than for children. Biologists already know the basic terminology and will feel patronized if you define terms like "mitochondria" and "fibril" for them. Other readers need more help and will resent each trip to the dictionary.

If you know the subject well, you'll assume that simply defining a word conveys the richness of a concept, but you'll be wrong. People need context and examples, and they finally understand only after the second or third explanation. If you under-explain, the reader will feel stupid and blame you for it.

Why write something that merely reviews what everyone already knows? Who needs a diet book that merely repeats the common wisdom of "exercise more and eat less?" If I buy a book on playing guitar, I want to learn how to hold my fingers, and why the strings buzz, not something that simply tells me to practice more. If I read an article on snakes, I want to learn more than that they have scales and are reptiles. Don't underestimate the intelligence of readers. If you don't really have anything new to say, learn something. Whatever you write will be unique, why not make sure you also have a unique message?

Only write about what interests you. If you are hired to write about something, get yourself interested or don't bother. You can't fool us. On the other hand, if you're truly interested in something, we will be too.

How interested are you in the sounds that dead trees make in the forest? I'm guessing not very. But Reg Saner is, and he talks about it a bit in his essay "Wind" collected in his book *Four Cornered Falcon*:

> But exhuberance won't get us past cold fact. "Face it," says fact; "Those voices you hear in wind aren't there." True, no matter how often I've heard dead trees cry. In thick forest that's a sound the wind makes: a dead trunk gets caught in its topple and is held, supported by living trunks which – for decades, as may happen – won't let that dead one fall, like our habit of taking along those

who couldn't make it. When wind tosses the living tree crowns, that grey trunk rubs audibly against them, as if a creature dismayed. It's my voice that makes it a creature. Ours. The kind of voice we humans lend things. Especially whatever sighs as it ends.

For that paragraph, I'm just as interested in the sounds of dead trees as the author.

When you're trying to teach something, nothing beats an accurate but vivid analogy. Drape your dusty concepts in colorful, easy-to-remember images. The boldest, most outrageous analogies stick best, but if they're too colorful, they'll seem funny. Luckily, most people enjoy an occasional bit of controlled humor. But if you'd rather not have your reader smile, keep your analogies chained within the safe parameters of your front lawn.

Most nonfiction writers don't have to worry about that. They keep their analogies locked in the basement and never let them see the light of day. A reader passing by on the street rarely hears their pitiful howling and remembers nothing. He'll be completely useless on the witness stand. "I'm sorry, Your Honor. Yes, I read the article, but I was daydreaming at the time. It was something about analogies ... " If you want to write traditional dull textbooks or committee reports, avoid interesting analogies. Once released, creative analogies will race to the sidewalk, jump all over your reader, whimper with joy and slobber on his face. That reader will never forget your message.

Trying it on Your Own

You don't need me or anyone else to examine and explain your favorite author's tricks. On the other hand, if the writer is skilled, you'll read an entire book and never notice they did anything. You'll get so caught up in the story or the information that if someone asks about it, you'll answer, no, they didn't do any of the things Kenn described. Active verbs? No, didn't especially notice them. Details? I don't know, I guess there were some details. Exaggeration? No, it all seemed about right. Unless you practice, you'll never see cards hidden up sleeves or the secret doorway at the back of the stage. That's what makes them good: they make you believe in their magic.

So you need to take a work you like and open it at random. Read a page somewhere in the middle so you won't get ensnared by the writer and therefore blind to her wiles. That's what I had to do for this book. I did not take careful notes of wonderful examples I could include. I simply opened good books at random to find my examples. It took about an hour to find them all, and it would have been quicker had not a couple of them captured me and forced me to read more. Good writers will do that to you if you let them.

Let's look at some examples of writing. Read the next paragraph once through to see if you like it or not. Then read it again trying to notice any little tricks the author might have used. Then I'll give you my reactions to it. This is from *Under the Tuscan Sun* by Frances Mayes:

> Big steaks sizzle over the huge bed of red coals. We join the long line and pick up our crostini, our plates and salad and vegetables. At the grill, our neighbor spears two enormous steaks for us and we lurch to a table already almost full. Pitchers of wine pass round and round. The whole town comes out for the sagra and, oddly, there seem to be no tourists here, except for a long table of English people. We don't know the people we're with. They're from Acquaviva. Two couples and three children. The baby girl is gnawing on a bone and looks delighted. The two boys, in the well-behaved way of Italian children, focus on sawing their steaks. The adults toast us and we toast back. When we say we're Americans, one man wants to know if we know his aunt and uncle in Chicago.

What is this author doing and do you like it or not? Well, first she's employing several senses. Steaks sizzle so we can *hear* them, and when they sizzle we can just about *smell* them too. The mention of specific foods engages our sense of *taste*. We *see* long tables.

Obviously she's playing the "senses" card this hand. But what else? She uses active verbs: steaks *sizzle*, the narrator *lurches*, pitchers of wine *pass*, babies *gnaw* on bones, little boys *saw* their steaks, adults *toast*. Sentences are short. Not all are complete. Of all the conversations that transpired, she chooses the detail of the couple asking if the narrator knows his relatives. This writer aggressively engages our senses, uses 75 percent active verbs, tends toward short sentences and chooses specific details carefully. If you enjoyed the paragraph, compare it with one of your own. If it's "too much" for you, that's good to know too.

That's what I want you to do. I want you to open books at random and dissect a few paragraphs. Determine what makes that particular writer tick, then decide if you want to imitate them or run the opposite direction.

I probably own different books than you do. Before you try this on your own, let me get a stack of books from my personal library, open each at random and pick a paragraph or so. You read it, determine if you like something about it, and try to figure out what it is. What compliment would you give each author? If you find nothing admirable in it, figure out what advice you'd give the author to improve. All these will be from published books by well-known authors. Each has many fans, several have won major prizes, some of the authors teach creative writing, but that doesn't matter. If you don't like something, notice it so you can avoid their mistake. In fairness, when you open a book at random you might not land on the writer's finest work and you might land on something intentionally dull or repetitive. Some selections may make you want to read more by that author. Others may warn you away. Writers tend to be consistent, page after page. I confess I knew what I'd find when I opened most of these books and articles.

There won't be a test, but I'll tell you this: I love some of the next examples, but I am apparently not the right reader to fully appreciate a couple of them. Even so, I can learn from them. They help me identify things I should stop doing. What can you learn from your reaction to each of these to shape your own writing?

Let's give it a try. *This is from Five-Finger Exercises, or What To Do Till the Muse Comes Back* by B.J. Chute

And there's more to Ebenezer Scrooge than an old man on a London street. Certainly Scrooge walks off the pages, but there must have been a time when he existed only in a writer's speculation. What did it take to make him come alive?

Words, just words. Not "just words," of course, but the right ones. They may have come easily or have been rewritten a dozen times; we don't know, and it doesn't matter. Ebenezer Scrooge is words on paper.

Dickens saw an old man – on the street or in the camera of his mind's eye. He could have described him as an old miser who had white hair and stubble on his chin, ate his meals alone in a dark room, was wholly indifferent to his fellow man, and was feared. A catalogue of simple facts, leaving the reader to draw the picture.

But, of course, Dickens did nothing of the kind. The "old miser" becomes that "covetous old sinner, hard and sharp as flint," who takes his gruel (not "meals," you notice) in a dark room; instead of "dark room," Dickens tells us that "Darkness is cheap, and Scrooge liked it," describing not only the darkness but the man himself. Nor does Dickens comment philosophically on Scrooge's uncaring attitude toward the needy; he lets Scrooge say it – "If they would rather die, they had better do it, and decrease the surplus population" – and the reader feels a cold shiver of revulsion.

The white hair and stubble become " A frosty rime was on his head, and on his eyebrows, and his wiry chin," conjuring up the miser's perpetual winter. And, as to his being feared, are we merely told that people are afraid of him? No, we are told that even the blind men's dogs, when they saw him coming, " would tug their owners into doorways and up courts."

Someone sent that one to me. I'd never read B. Joy Chute but, after reading that passage, I looked up her books to buy. Eighty percent active verbs, crisp short sentences, excellent choice of details. The choice of details to illustrate the point may be the feature that most impresses me. How about you? What did you like or dislike?

This next one is by Donovan Hohn in an article titled "A Romance of Rust" in the January 2005 edition of *Harpers Magazine*:

> ... I walked among fabulous machines as small as schnauzers and as huge as elephants, all gleaming in the August sun. Drive belts whirred, flywheels revolved, pistons fired, and a forest of smokestacks piped foul smoke and rude music into the otherwise cloudless sky. Mostly, I have ridden a Midwestern circuit of flea markets and farm auctions in the passenger seat of an emerald green Toyota pickup truck piloted by a fifty-five year old botanist with a ponytail, spectacles like windowpanes, and a beard verging on the Whitmanesque.

You know what I'd say if I were reading this like a writer. I'd look at active verbs, use of analogy, choice of details, sentence length, use of modifiers. I'd have an opinion about each. But what do you think?

If you aren't yet thinking of your own reactions to these, I have failed my mission. Read the examples and develop your own opinion about them before you read mine.

Opening at random *Doctor Hudson's Secret Journal* by Lloyd C Douglass I see the following exchange. Do you like the way the author handles dialog? Why or why not?

> There was a little pause before Dorothy inquired, with blue eyes wide, "Where do hunches come from?"
>
> I toyed with my watch-chain and smiled ineffectively.
>
> "I've noticed that whenever you're stuck,"

drawled Dorothy, with the bland impudence of a five-year-old, "you begin to wonder what time it is. Does that watch trick of yours mean that you want to get rid of me; or, do you do that when you're alone – and stuck?"

Never having examined myself on this matter before, I hesitated in replying, a chink she promptly filled with "But maybe you're never stuck – when you're alone." And when I failed to answer quickly she added, "Are you?"

When you read that, do any word tricks leap out at you? For example, do you notice the active verbs or not? Does the vocabulary seem old fashioned or pompous, or do you enjoy less-ordinary words like bland, impudence, and chink? Did you notice the way the little girl starts speaking in the middle of the last paragraph? Does that intensify the feeling that she's interrupting, not giving him time to respond? Or was it a coincidence?

Here are the first lines of *The Poisonwood Bible* by Barbara Kingsolver:

Imagine a ruin so strange it must never have happened.

First, picture the forest. I want you to be its conscience, the eyes in the trees. The trees are columns of slick, brindled bark like muscular animals overgrown beyond all reason. Every space is filled with life: delicate, poisonous frogs war-painted like skeletons, clutched in copulation, secreting their precious eggs onto dripping leaves. Vines strangling their own kin in the everlasting wrestle for sunlight. The breathing of monkeys. A glide of snake belly on branch. A single-file army of ants biting a mammoth tree into uniform grains and hauling it down to the dark for their ravenous queen. And, in reply, a choir of seedlings arching their necks out of rotted tree stumps, sucking life out of death. This forest eats itself and lives forever.

Did you notice anything interesting about the point of view? It's in the second person, just like this paragraph is. She's talking to you, the reader, directly as if writing a letter. Did that work for you? What else did you notice? Did incomplete sentences bother you? Not me.

I opened *The Diary of Samuel Pepys* at random and my eye fell on this entry, dated September 29, 1662. I'm not sure what it illustrates, but it made me smile:

> (Michaelmas day). This day my oaths for drinking of wine and going to plays are out, and so I do resolve to take a liberty today, and then to fall to them again. To the King's Theatre, where we saw "Midsummer's Night's Dream," which I had never seen before, nor shall ever again, for it is the most insipid ridiculous play that ever I saw in my life. I saw, I confess, some good dancing and some handsome women, and which was all my pleasure.

What made me smile at that? Listening to this curmudgeon whine about one of the most successful plays in history (an experience made tolerable only because of the pretty women) we get a clear image of the speaker. He has strong opinions and isn't shy about expressing them. Four hundred years later, I can still picture him scribbling this in his journal. Maybe I should consider giving my characters some strong opinions.

Opening *I Know This Much is True* by Wally Lamb I find this:

> I was outside in front, waiting on the wall when Leo pulled up in his Skylark.
> I threw my fishing gear in the backseat and got in the front. "Here," I said, tossing him one of the foil-wrapped eggplant grinders Ma had made me the night before. "Present from my mother."
> "See that, Birdsey," he said. "Even the older babes love me. When you got it, you got it." Ma a babe? I had to laugh in spite of my headache, and the mess I'd

made with Dessa, and the fight I'd just had with my stupid, whacked-out brother.

I like that the characters reveal so much by what they say and what they think. We find out Leo has a high opinion of himself, that the narrator has a headache, made a mess with Dessa, had a fight with her brother, and can't imagine anyone thinking her (or his) mother attractive. We learn all that from thoughts and dialog, not narration. Interesting.

This is from Dave Barry (who I always reverently refer to as "Pulitzer Prize Winning/New York Times Bestselling author Mr. Dave Barry") in his book *Dave Barry in Cyberspace*:

> I could go on and on, listing the ways in which computers enrich our everyday lives. But I've made my point, which is that we live in the Computer Age, and *you need to get with the program*. You are standing in the airport terminal of life, and the jet plane of the 21st century is about to take off. You must make a choice: Do you remain in the terminal, eating the stale vending-machine food of outmoded thinking? Or do you get on the plane and soar into the stratosphere of computerization, swept along by the jet stream of evolving technology, enjoying the in-flight snack of virtually unlimited information access, secure in the knowledge that if you encounter the turbulence of rapid change, you are holding, in this book, the barf bag of expert guidance?

Please note that Mr. Barry's final sentence refers, almost certainly, to his own book *Dave Barry In Cyberspace* and not this one, the one you are *really* holding, which is *Joy Writing*. This book does not even aspire to being the barf bag of expert guidance. But speaking of that, did you happen to notice any analogies in his work?

Here's a paragraph from *The Color of Law* by David Milofski:

Andy paused. The audience was restless, and he didn't want to lose them. "I was going to read this statement," he said, indicating his notes. "But I don't really think this is the venue for speeches, at least not from me. It's a time for conscience, and we must all attend to those demands as best we can. I know I will. I do want to say that, like Reverend Jackson, I am concerned that Mayor Mueller and Chief Tanner do not believe this tragedy is worthy of their attention. Unfortunately, this is not an isolated incident and those in positions of responsibility should address publicly any questions regarding the conduct of Milwaukee police officers. I too find it very peculiar that no investigation has been authorized into the alleged conspiracy to cover up the actions of those officers involved in the death of Jimmy Norman."

What do you think about that? What do you like or dislike? Can you distinguish your feelings toward the character from your feelings about the writer?

This is from *The Known World* by Edward P. Jones:

Travis said nothing but shook Skiffington's hand and collected his children and went down and over the rise. He still had some of the $15 he had received for the cow, but it would not give him the pleasure he had known before he learned that the cow had another life. Skiffington watched him. Travis had a child on either side of him, both with their black Cherokee hair flowing and both almost as dark as their mother. One of Travis's children looked up and said something to Travis and Travis, before they all disappeared, looked down to answer the child, the man's head seeming to go down in small stages, heavy with bitterness. The boy nodded at whatever his father had told him.

Good writer? Bad writer? Someone to copy? Why do you feel that way? Does the fact that he won a Pulitzer for that book affect your opinion? When I read it, I notice that the rhythm of the sentences seems distinctive, and somehow different from other examples we've used. Read it out loud and see if you agree. I wonder what he's doing that makes me feel that way?

This is from *Think Like a Billionaire* by Donald Trump:

> If you play a lot of golf, your game will improve with time. Cary Stephan, the golf pro at the Trump National Golf Club in Briarcliff Manor, New York, feels that good golfers need to put in two to three hours per week of practice – whether it's on the putting green, or playing rounds, or at the driving range. Serious golfers looking to improve their game should devote an hour a week to instruction. Golf, like everything else in life, requires dedication.
>
> The rest is pure talent. I recently played golf with Annika Sorenstam, the Swedish golf champion, at the Trump National Golf Club in Briarcliff Manor. Hard as I try to be fair about the fairer sex, I still don't like being outdriven by a woman. After playing with Annika, I have to say that I'm happy I'm in the real estate business. I did, however, ask her how she does what she does so well. Her answer reminded me of Babe Ruth's: "I just do it." Basically, she works hard, but she's got great talent.

What's your reaction? Do you want to become Trump's writing apprentice, or do we need to say, "Sorry, Don, you're fired." What does he do that you'd like to copy, or what would you change? Did you notice his use of repetition? Did it create emphasis, or seem accidental to you? I can hear Mr. Trump's voice in these lines; it sounds like him talking. If he conveyed the information more concisely, he might lose some of that conversational feeling, but then we'd have fewer words doing the same job. You need to decide for yourself how you'd feel about that choice.

This is from *Sick Puppy* by Carl Hiaasen:

> On the morning of April 24, an hour past dawn, a man named Palmer Stoat shot a rare African black rhinoceros. He fired from a distance of thirteen yards and used a Winchester .458, which knocked him flat on his back. The rhinoceros wheeled, as if to charge, before snorting twice and sagging to its knees. Its head came to rest under a spread of palmettos.
>
> Palmer Stoat instructed his guide, a former feed salesman named Durgess, to unpack the camera.
>
> "Let's first make sure she's dead," Durgess said.

What strikes you about that? Sentence length? Detail? Active verbs? Does he make us curious? Does it seem like he's extraordinarily efficient, including lots of information and detail in few words? Do you know what to picture when he says "palmetto?" If not, does that bother you? I don't know what a palmetto is, but it didn't slow me down. It made me feel like I'm in an exotic locale where there will be many plants I can't name, and I'm willing to live with that for a while. Interesting. An unfamiliar word makes the location seem exotic. I'll have to remember that.

This is from *Harm's Way* by Stephen White:

> Then there was her marriage.
>
> Her relationship with Peter had always been the anomaly in Adrienne's life. Peter didn't need her, at least not in any conventional manner that I ever discerned. She knew she wasn't indispensable to him, never had been, never would be, and that fact left her teetering on the edge of an awkward emotional vertigo with him. I suspected that the lack of equilibrium was the foundation of their attraction for each other; they kept each other off balance in a way that was peculiar and addictive. The whole affair, I'd decided, was the romantic equivalent of Peter's love for rock-climbing – free-soloing – a death defying act of scaling great affectional heights without ropes or safety equipment.

The relationship he describes is so odd to the writer that he struggles to explain it, desperately seeking some kind of analogy that fits. They have reached a kind of dynamic balance – yes, the writer exclaims, that's it. An uneasy, dangerous give-and-take that's similar to the danger, fear, and attraction of rock climbing. It's an unusual love, an unusual relationship, and the only way to describe it is with an unusual metaphor. Maybe next time I have to describe something unusual, I'll consider an unusual metaphor, some connection that most wouldn't make.

The first lines of *Pillars of the Earth* by Ken Follett :

> The small boys came early to the hanging.
> It was still dark when the first three or four of them sidled out of the hovels, quiet as cats in their felt boots. A thin layer of fresh snow covered the little town like a new coat of paint, and theirs were the first footprints to blemish its perfect surface. They picked their way through the huddled wooden huts and along the streets of frozen mud to the silent marketplace, where the gallows stood waiting.

The first sentence alone makes us curious. He employs several choice active verbs: sidled, blemish, picked. Carefully selected details provide both atmosphere and information. We know it's winter, for example, without spending words to say it. He uses several senses: "quiet" and "silent" address our sense of hearing; "frozen" involves our sense of touch; the snow, the dark, the gallows all appeal to our sense of sight. He uses anthropomorphosis: the gallows stood waiting; huddled wooden huts. He uses simile: "quiet as cats," "like a new coat of paint."

From *Brightness Falls* by Jay McInerney:

> Trailing shirttails and shoelaces, Jeff appeared in Russell's office as if from bed, his shirt more frayed than usual, the button-down collar unbuttoned and upturned, knees showing through his ripped chinos. Only the blue blazer imparted a precarious note of formality. Adjusting

the bill of his cap, inscribed with the motto "Save Me from What I Want," he disheveled himself onto Russell's couch and plucked the Post from Russell's desk "'Wild Cat Terrorizes City,'" he read.

"Who is this person," Russell asked Donna

"Your lunch date."

"Your meal ticket, actually," Jeff said.

This is from *Singing in the Comeback Choir*, by Bebe Moore Campbell:

Miles Davis's trumpet soared into high notes just as Lindy slapped down an ace of diamonds on the ten on her kitchen table. She picked up both cards. "How do you like that, Bootsy?" she asked gleefully as she raked a small pile of cards toward her.

"You think you really something," her opponent said good-naturedly. He filled the kitchen with the scent of Old Spice and the liveliness of his smile. "I know you cheated, woman." It was what he usually said when she won. Lindy gave Bootsy the laugh he was looking for.

Did the author use details? Senses? Active verbs?

Now go to your own favorite books. You know what things interest me, but more importantly you know what little tricks resonate with you. See what your own favorite authors choose.

Repetition reinforces. This can be good or bad. People tend to repeat things they feel strongly:

> "I can't believe you did that!" he said. "I just can't believe you did it."

When humans hear repetition, we don't understand the speaker's message any better, but we feel his conviction. Writers take advantage of this unstated communication pattern by restating important ideas.

When Robert Frost got to the core of his poem, he wrote:

> But I have promises to keep,
> And miles to go before I sleep,
> And miles to go before I sleep.

This feels much different than, "I have many miles to go before I sleep."

The principal of investing something with meaning by repetition carries beyond simply saying things twice. Readers deduce that a locket holds special meaning for a character if he looks at it often. If he blushes when any girl walks by, we understand he's shy. If he only blushes for one girl, but does so six times, he's in love.

The danger is this: repetition suggests importance, whether we mean it to or not. If a character falls asleep at the end of every chapter, readers decide he's got a sleep disorder. If the moon is always mysterious, readers get nervous whenever it's shining, wondering why no one let them in on the mystery. While reading this book, did you decide I'm a fan of John Steinbeck, or any other writer, because I used more than one example of their writing? Or am I so crafty I did that intentionally, just to illustrate this point?

Restating concepts reinforces them. To emphasize a point, repeat it. When teaching, you need to repeat each concept several times before a reader fully owns it. Therefore, let me repeat the things we have discussed in this book:

Let yourself write badly when you create first drafts, and don't show that bad writing to anyone. Resist the impulse to edit as you go.

When you revise, eliminate clutter and write simply. Use active verbs and specific nouns. Be nervous about adjectives and adverbs. Don't weaken verbs with limiters like "sort of" or "a little." Don't try to pump up weak verbs with generic modifiers like "very."

Consider the ideas that feel important to you, and let your writing convey them. Create curiosity. Begin at the beginning. Show, don't tell. Use the words you love but avoid pretension. Encourage the reader to become an active participant. Choose details wisely, enlist the senses, create analogies. Write boldly, revise relentlessly. Practice.

Most important, read a lot, notice techniques that work for you, and try to incorporate them into your own writing. Read like a detective looking for clues or an apprentice watching a master magician. Then pull your own unique rabbits from your chosen hat.

Write for the joy of writing. Don't write for a teacher, friend, critique group, or editor. The more personal the writing, the more universal it will be. Express the things you feel deeply about. That's what will bring you the greatest satisfaction, what will make your writing significant, and what will captivate readers.

Write for the joy of writing.

Epilog

After writing many partial books, dozens of essays and short stories, and hundreds of songs and poems, I finally finished a science fiction novel and began submitting it to agents and publishers. After twenty-eight rejections, I decided it just wasn't good enough so I put it into a drawer and started to write *There Are No Electrons: Electronics for Earthlings*. I took some writing courses, read a bunch of books, subscribed to writing magazines, went to writers conferences, joined a writers club and a critique group.

Experts said that editors favored authors with many publishing credits. To acquire these, I started sending out poems. I had boxes full of them, they required little typing, postage was cheap, and a credit was a credit.

I kept a log-book of my submissions and sent out at least three poems each and every day. When they came back rejected, I sent them back out within twenty-four hours. I wanted to have statistics working for me instead of against me.

Because of the log-book, the process became data I could analyze. On average, I sent out twenty-five groups of three poems for each poem accepted. As I got better at picking magazines, my average improved to 9 rejections per acceptance, or twenty-seven individual poems rejected for each one accepted.

Over fifty of my poems were accepted and published.

Back cover quotes or "blurbs" by well-known writers were supposed to impress editors, so I went to the local library and spent hours tracking down contact information. I sent out forty packages to my favorite authors. Four responded with wonderful blurbs: Dave Barry, Ray Bradbury, Clive Cussler, and George Garrett. These gentlemen are saints, please buy everything they write.

Unfortunately, blurbs and credits did nothing to help the sale of *There Are No Electrons*. It was rejected eighty-nine times by editors and agents before I decided they were all wrong. The book was better than that. People liked it, I felt there was a market. So I bought Dan Poynter's book *The Self Publishing Manual* to learn if it might be feasible to do it myself. Sure, I had no money and no experience in publishing, but what harm could come of educating myself? I decided to take all the steps I could to self-publish and would only stop when I reached an insurmountable step, like when I had to write out a check. I learned a bit about book design, bartered with freelance editors, got printing bids and became increasingly excited. When it was time to write out the check, miraculously, the money appeared. I printed 500 copies.

Having no money to advertise, I sent out 100 copies to newspapers and magazines for review. Ninety-nine managed to ignore the book completely, but one magazine reviewed it in glowing terms. Unfortunately, the magazine only circulated in Southern California, and I couldn't get a single book store or distributor in Southern California to carry the book. So the review resulted in no sales.

Belatedly, I persuaded several wholesalers to enter the book into their databases so, if someone ordered one, they could get it. Then I sent out another 100 review copies, this time to smaller magazines and specialized markets. Ninety-eight found it unworthy of mention, but two liked it. One, a fabulous review in *Radio and Electronics* magazine, caused people all over the country to go to their local bookstore asking for the book. Suddenly, distributors were calling me, bookstores faxed orders, and I sold out the rest of the printing. Part of me thought I should be grateful to escape without losing money and quit. The other part thought I should reprint and keep plugging away. That's what I did.

There Are No Electrons has been paying my mortgage for fifteen years now and continues to sell well. All the editors who rejected it were, in fact, wrong. Many subsequently called saying they'd changed their minds. Now that it was selling well, if I'd accept a small advance, they'd be willing to gamble on the book. I rejected them all.

Because of that book's success, I was able to spend a year learning algebra so I could write *Algebra Unplugged* with Jim Loats, a math professor. That led to a three-year project of learning calculus and writing *Calculus for Cats,* again with Jim, and also the publication of one of my novels, *The Land of Debris and the Home of Alfredo.* Each found an audience.

I get cool fan mail, meet wonderful people, and make a reasonable living as a result of writing. I feel I've been extraordinarily lucky.

I'd like for you to be lucky as well. In most ways, we aren't competitors. You and I will never duel over the same phrase; you're not likely to write a funny book that teaches electronics; I'm unlikely to attempt writing the history of your great aunt Phaedra. If they concede writing math books to me, I'll concede vampires to Ann Rice and the word "utterly" to Annie Dillard. Writing is a celebration in a large tent with room for everyone. We belong to a huge, gloriously happy, and diverse family.

Getting published, on the other hand, is hard work.

You've heard the cliché, "opportunity only knocks once." In my world, opportunity answers the door for the guy who just keeps knocking. Smart beats lucky every time and persistence beats them both. Go to your library and ask the reference librarian to steer you toward books about publishing and books that list publishers. Submit your work only to publishers that publish the kind of book, poem, essay, or poetry you've got. Duh! Subscribe to writers' magazines, join a group. Educate yourself about the business. Expect to be rejected a huge percentage of the time. Don't take it personally. Make statistics work in your favor.

As far as getting your words published, I *am* your competition. If you're only willing to be rejected a dozen times or so, even if you're twice the writer I am, I will eat you alive.

Consider yourself warned.

This book quotes from the following sources. We thank the authors and copyright owners for the use of their words. With the exception of the quotations that are extremely short and also fit the other criteria of "fair usage" and those that reside within the public domain, the copyright owners have given us permission to reprint these excerpts. We've tried to contact each copyright owner, regardless of the brevity of the quote, and also the living authors represented. Special thanks to those authors who gave us specific permission to quote them.